THE COMPLETE DIABETES CANNING RECIPE BOOK FOR BEGINNERS

Everything You Need to Know About Healthy Preservation Methods for Low-Sugar, Diabetic-Friendly Foods to Maintain a Healthy Lifestyle

Steve Bryant, MD, RD

Copyright Page

Table of Contents

Introduction to the World of Diabetes Canning

D iabetes mellitus refers to a group of diseases that affect how the body uses blood sugar (glucose). Glucose is an important source of energy for the cells that make up the muscles and tissues. It's also the brain's main source of fuel.

The main cause of diabetes varies by type. But no matter what type of diabetes you have, it can lead to excess sugar in the blood. Too much sugar in the blood can lead to serious health problems.

Chronic diabetes conditions include type 1 diabetes and type 2 diabetes. Potentially reversible diabetes conditions include prediabetes and gestational diabetes. Prediabetes happens when blood sugar levels are higher than normal. But the blood sugar levels aren't high enough to be called diabetes. And prediabetes can lead to diabetes unless steps are taken to prevent it. Gestational diabetes happens during pregnancy. But it may go away after the baby is born.

Chapter 1: A Look at Type 1 & 2 diabetes

Type 1 diabetes, once known as juvenile diabetes or insulin-dependent diabetes, is a chronic condition. In this condition, the pancreas makes little or no insulin.

Insulin is a hormone responsible for breaking down the sugar in the blood for use throughout the body. A person living with type 1 diabetes may receive a diagnosis during childhood.

Different factors, such as genetics and some viruses, may cause type 1 diabetes. Although type 1 diabetes usually appears during childhood or adolescence, it can develop in adults.

People living with type 1 diabetes need to regularly administer insulin. Individuals may do this with injections or an insulin pump.

Even after a lot of research, type 1 diabetes has no cure. Treatment is directed toward managing the amount of sugar in the blood using insulin, diet and lifestyle to prevent complications.

Once a person receives their diagnosis, they need to regularly monitor their blood sugar levels, administer insulin, and follow some lifestyle strategies to help manage the condition.

Successfully managing blood sugar levels can help people living with type 1 diabetes avoid serious complications.

Type 1 diabetes vs. secondary diabetes

A condition called secondary diabetes is like type 1, but your insulin-making cells are wiped out by another health condition or an injury to your pancreas, rather than by your immune system.

Type 1 diabetes vs. type 2 diabetes

If you have type 1, your body doesn't make enough insulin. With type 2 diabetes, your body can make insulin but can't use it well. The cells in your muscles, fat, and liver build up what's called insulin resistance.

With type 1 diabetes, you need to use man-made insulin every day so your body can function. But not everyone with type 2 diabetes needs it. Other medications can help you manage the condition.

No matter which type of diabetes you have, you'll need to keep a close eye on your daily habits, such as what you eat and how much activity you get to stay healthy.

Causes and Risk Factors of Type 1 Diabetes

The exact cause of type 1 diabetes is unknown. Usually, the body's own immune system — which normally fights harmful bacteria and viruses — destroys the insulin-producing (islet) cells in the pancreas. Other possible causes include:

• Genetics

• Exposure to viruses and other environmental factors

The role of insulin

Once a large number of islet cells are destroyed, the body will produce little or no insulin. Insulin is a hormone that comes from a gland behind and below the stomach (pancreas).

• The pancreas puts insulin into the bloodstream.

• Insulin travels through the body, allowing sugar to enter the cells.

• Insulin lowers the amount of sugar in the bloodstream.

• As the blood sugar level drops, the pancreas puts less insulin into the bloodstream.

The role of glucose

Glucose — a sugar — is a main source of energy for the cells that make up muscles and other tissues.

• Glucose comes from two major sources: food and the liver.

• Sugar is absorbed into the bloodstream, where it enters cells with the help of insulin.

• The liver stores glucose in the form of glycogen.

• When glucose levels are low, such as when you haven't eaten in a while, the liver breaks down the stored glycogen into glucose. This keeps glucose levels within a typical range.

In type 1 diabetes, there's no insulin to let glucose into the cells. Because of this, sugar builds up in the bloodstream. This can cause life-threatening complications.

Risk factors

Some factors that can raise your risk for type 1 diabetes include:

• **Family history.** Anyone with a parent or sibling with type 1 diabetes has a slightly higher risk of developing the condition.

• **Genetics.** Having certain genes increases the risk of developing type 1 diabetes.

• **Geography.** The number of people who have type 1 diabetes tends to be higher as you travel away from the equator.

• **Age.** Type 1 diabetes can appear at any age, but it appears at two noticeable peaks. The first peak occurs in children between 4 and 7 years old. The second is in children between 10 and 14 years old.

Symptoms and Diagnosis of Type 1 Diabetes

Diabetes symptoms depend on how high your blood sugar is. Some people, especially if they have prediabetes, gestational diabetes or type 2 diabetes, may not have symptoms. In type 1 diabetes, symptoms tend to come on quickly and be more severe.

Some of the symptoms of type 1 diabetes and type 2 diabetes are:

• Feeling more thirsty than usual.

• Urinating often.

• Losing weight without trying.

• Presence of ketones in the urine. Ketones are a byproduct of the breakdown of muscle and fat that happens when there's not enough available insulin.

• Feeling tired and weak.

• Feeling irritable or having other mood changes.

• Having blurry vision.

• Having slow-healing sores.

• Getting a lot of infections, such as gum, skin and vaginal infections.

Type 1 Diabetes in Children

Your child is at higher risk of type 1 diabetes if:

- They're aged 4-6 years or 10-14 years.

- Another family member also has it.

Type 1 diabetes symptoms in children

The signs are the same as for adults, but you may also notice:

- More diaper changes for a baby

- Diaper rash that doesn't get better when treated

- Bed-wetting in kids who are potty-trained

- Fast breathing

- Belly pain

- Throwing up

• Behavior changes

• Fruity-smelling breath

In some babies or kids, type 1 diabetes can also look like the flu.

If you notice any of these symptoms, take your child to the doctor.

Late-onset type 1 diabetes symptoms

• More research is being done on what's called Latent Autoimmune Diabetes in Adults (LADA). Some people refer to this as "Diabetes 1.5" or "Diabetes 1 1/2" because it overlaps with parts of both type 1 and type 2 diabetes.

• LADA symptoms can come on very slowly, making it tricky to diagnose. So does the fact that people who have it are usually at a healthy weight, and often between the ages of 30 and 50 years.

Type 1 Diabetes Diagnosis

If your doctor thinks you have type 1 diabetes, they'll check your blood sugar levels. This can be done in a few different ways.

A1c test. Also called a glycated hemoglobin test, it can figure out your average blood sugar levels over the past 3 months with one small blood sample. It does that by counting the number of hemoglobin (red blood) cells that are sticky with glucose.

If your A1c result is 6.5% or higher, you'll retake the test. If it's the same number or higher, you likely have diabetes.

This test may not give you a correct result if you have any of the following:

• Pregnancy

• Kidney failure

• Liver disease

• Severe anemia

• Blood loss

• Some blood disorders, such as sickle cell anemia

• Certain medicines, such as HIV drugs, in your system

If you're of African, Mediterranean, or Southeast Asian descent, you could also have a different type of hemoglobin (called a hemoglobin variant) that could skew your A1c result. Let your doctor know if any of these apply to you. If so, they can test your blood sugar in different ways, such as

Fasting blood sugar test. In this test, your blood's taken after you haven't eaten overnight. A result of 126 milligrams per deciliter (mg/dL) or higher on two separate tests signals diabetes.

Random blood sugar test. Your blood glucose can also be checked at a random time. Whether or not you've recently eaten, a result of 200 mg/dL or higher means diabetes.

Type 1 diabetes test

The above tests can show whether you have diabetes, but they can't tell you which type. To find out whether you have type 1 or type 2 diabetes, your doctor will need to look for:

Autoantibodies. These are the proteins in your immune system that attack healthy cells, such as beta cells in your pancreas that make insulin. If you have type 1 diabetes, they'll show up in a blood sample.

Ketones. When you have type 1, your body relies on acids called ketones for fuel because it doesn't have enough glucose to use. A urine (pee) test can detect them.

Complications of Type 1 Diabetes

Over time, type 1 diabetes complications can affect major organs in the body. These organs include the heart, blood vessels, nerves, eyes and kidneys. Having a normal blood sugar level can lower the risk of many complications.

Diabetes complications can lead to disabilities or even threaten your life.

• **Heart and blood vessel disease.** Diabetes increases the risk of some problems with the heart and blood vessels. These include coronary artery disease with chest pain (angina), heart attack, stroke, narrowing of the arteries (atherosclerosis) and high blood pressure.

• **Nerve damage (neuropathy).** Too much sugar in the blood can injure the walls of the tiny blood vessels (capillaries) that feed the nerves. This is especially true in the legs. This can cause tingling, numbness, burning or pain. This usually begins at the tips of the toes or fingers and spreads upward. Poorly controlled blood sugar could cause you to lose all sense of feeling in the affected limbs over time.

Damage to the nerves that affect the digestive system can cause problems with nausea, vomiting, diarrhea or constipation. For men, erectile dysfunction may be an issue.

• **Kidney damage (nephropathy).** The kidneys have millions of tiny blood vessels that keep waste from entering the blood. Diabetes can damage this system. Severe damage can lead to kidney failure or end-stage kidney disease that can't be reversed. End-stage kidney disease needs to be treated with mechanical filtering of the kidneys (dialysis) or a kidney transplant.

• **Eye damage.** Diabetes can damage the blood vessels in the retina (part of the eye that senses light) (diabetic retinopathy). This could cause blindness. Diabetes also increases the risk of other serious vision conditions, such as cataracts and glaucoma.

• **Foot damage.** Nerve damage in the feet or poor blood flow to the feet increases the risk of some foot complications. Left untreated, cuts and blisters can become serious infections. These infections may need to be treated with toe, foot or leg removal (amputation).

• **Skin and mouth conditions.** Diabetes may leave you more prone to infections of the skin and mouth. These include bacterial and fungal infections. Gum disease and dry mouth also are more likely.

• **Pregnancy complications.** High blood sugar levels can be dangerous for both the parent and the baby. The risk of miscarriage, stillbirth and birth defects increases when diabetes isn't well-controlled. For the parent, diabetes increases the risk of diabetic ketoacidosis, diabetic eye problems (retinopathy), pregnancy-induced high blood pressure and preeclampsia.

Treatment of Type 1 Diabetes

Treatment for type 1 diabetes includes:

• Taking insulin

• Counting carbohydrates, fats and protein

• Monitoring blood sugar often

- Eating healthy foods

- Exercising regularly and keeping a healthy weight

The goal is to keep the blood sugar level as close to normal as possible to delay or prevent complications. Generally, the goal is to keep the daytime blood sugar levels before meals between 80 and 130 mg/dL (4.44 to 7.2 mmol/L). After-meal numbers should be no higher than 180 mg/dL (10 mmol/L) two hours after eating.

Insulin and other medications

Anyone who has type 1 diabetes needs insulin therapy throughout their life.

There are many types of insulin, including:

• **Short-acting insulin.** Sometimes called regular insulin, this type starts working around 30 minutes after injection. It reaches peak effect at 90 to 120 minutes and lasts about 4 to 6 hours. Examples are Humulin R, Novolin R and Afrezza.

• **Rapid-acting insulin.** This type of insulin starts working within 15 minutes. It reaches peak effect at 60 minutes and lasts about 4 hours. This type is often used 15 to 20 minutes before meals. Examples are glulisine (Apidra), lispro (Humalog, Admelog and Lyumjev) and aspart (Novolog and FiAsp).

• **Intermediate-acting insulin.** Also called NPH insulin, this type of insulin starts working in about 1 to 3 hours. It reaches peak effect at 6 to 8 hours and lasts 12 to 24 hours. Examples are insulin NPH (Novolin N, Humulin N).

- **Long- and ultra-long-acting insulin**. This type of insulin may provide coverage for as long as 14 to 40 hours. Examples are glargine (Lantus, Toujeo Solostar, Basaglar), detemir (Levemir) and degludec (Tresiba).

You'll probably need several daily injections that include a combination of a long-acting insulin and a rapid-acting insulin. These injections act more like the body's normal use of insulin than do older insulin regimens that only required one or two shots a day. A combination of three or more insulin injections a day has been shown to improve blood sugar levels.

Insulin delivery options

Insulin can't be taken by mouth to lower blood sugar because stomach enzymes will break down the insulin, preventing it from working. You'll need to either get shots (injections) or use an insulin pump.

• **Injections.** You can use a fine needle and syringe or an insulin pen to inject insulin under the skin. Insulin pens look like ink pens and are available in disposable or refillable varieties.

If you choose shots (injections), you'll probably need a mixture of insulin types to use during the day and night.

• **An insulin pump.** This is a small device worn on the outside of your body that you program to deliver specific amounts of insulin throughout the day and when you eat. A tube connects a reservoir of insulin to a catheter that's inserted under the skin of your abdomen.

There's also a tubeless pump option that involves wearing a pod containing the insulin on your body combined with a tiny catheter that's inserted under your skin.

Blood sugar monitoring

Depending on the type of insulin therapy you select or need, you may have to check and record your blood sugar level at least four times a day.

The American Diabetes Association recommends testing blood sugar levels before meals and snacks, before bed, before exercising or driving, and whenever you think you have low blood sugar. Careful monitoring is the only way to make sure that your blood sugar level remains within your target range. More frequent monitoring can lower A1C levels.

Even if you take insulin and eat on a strict schedule, blood sugar levels can change. You'll learn how your blood sugar level changes in response to food, activity, illness, medications, stress, hormonal changes and alcohol.

Continuous glucose monitoring

Continuous glucose monitoring (CGM) monitors blood sugar levels. It may be especially helpful for preventing low blood sugar. These devices have been shown to lower A1C.

Continuous glucose monitors attach to the body using a fine needle just under the skin. They check blood glucose levels every few minutes.

Closed loop system

A closed loop system is a device implanted in the body that links a continuous glucose monitor to an insulin pump. The monitor checks blood sugar levels regularly. The device automatically delivers the right amount of insulin when the monitor shows that it's needed.

The Food and Drug Administration has approved several hybrid closed loop systems for type 1 diabetes. They are called "hybrid" because these systems require some input from the user. For example, you may have to tell the device how many carbohydrates are eaten, or confirm blood sugar levels from time to time.

A closed loop system that doesn't need any user input isn't available yet. But more of these systems currently are in clinical trials.

Other medications

Other medications also may be prescribed for people with type 1 diabetes, such as:

• **High blood pressure medications.** Your provider may prescribe angiotensin-converting enzyme (ACE) inhibitors or angiotensin II receptor blockers (ARBs) to help keep your kidneys healthy. These medications are recommended for people with diabetes who have blood pressures above 140/90 millimeters of mercury (mm Hg).

• **Aspirin.** Your provider may recommend you take baby or regular aspirin daily to protect your heart. Your provider may feel that you have an increased risk of a cardiovascular event. Your provider will discuss the risk of bleeding if you take aspirin.

- **Cholesterol-lowering drugs.** Cholesterol guidelines are stricter for people with diabetes because of their higher risk of heart disease.

The American Diabetes Association recommends that low-density lipoprotein (LDL, or "bad") cholesterol be below 100 mg/dL (2.6 mmol/L). High-density lipoprotein (HDL, or "good") cholesterol is recommended to be over 50 mg/dL (1.3 mmol/L) in women and over 40 mg/dL (1 mmol/L) in men. Triglycerides, another type of blood fat, should be less than 150 mg/dL (1.7 mmol/L).

Overview of Type 2 Diabetes

Type 2 diabetes is a condition that happens because of a problem in the way the body regulates and uses sugar as a fuel. That sugar also is called glucose. This long-term condition results in too much sugar circulating in the blood. Eventually, high blood sugar levels can lead to disorders of the circulatory, nervous and immune systems.

In type 2 diabetes, there are primarily two problems. The pancreas does not produce enough insulin — a hormone that regulates the movement of sugar into the cells. And cells respond poorly to insulin and take in less sugar. Healthy blood sugar (glucose) levels are 70 to 99 milligrams per deciliter (mg/dL). If you have undiagnosed Type 2 diabetes, your levels are typically 126 mg/dL or higher.

Type 2 diabetes used to be known as adult-onset diabetes, but both type 1 and type 2 diabetes can begin during childhood and adulthood. Type 2 is more common in older adults. But the increase in the number of children with obesity has led to more cases of type 2 diabetes in younger people. Uncontrolled type 2 diabetes can lead to chronically high blood glucose levels, which can cause several symptoms and potentially lead to serious complications.

Type 2 is the most common form of diabetes. About 1 in 10 people in the U.S. have type 2. Nearly 1 in 3 have prediabetes, meaning their blood sugar (or blood glucose) is high but not high enough to be diabetes yet.

There's no cure for type 2 diabetes. Losing weight, eating well and exercising can help manage the disease. If diet and exercise aren't enough to control blood sugar, diabetes medications or insulin therapy may be recommended.

Stages of Type 2 Diabetes

Researchers have defined four stages of type 2 diabetes:

Insulin resistance

In this stage, your body usually makes enough insulin to keep blood sugar levels in the normal range. But if your cells "resist" the insulin (don't use it correctly), your body will make more insulin to try to help the glucose get into them. Insulin resistance can be temporary, but it can also last.

There's no test to detect insulin resistance, so it can be hard to diagnose.

Prediabetes

Eventually, insulin resistance causes glucose to build up in your blood. You have prediabetes when your blood sugar levels are higher than normal, but not high enough to be considered diabetes. An A1c between 5.7% and 6.4% means you have prediabetes. You may not have any symptoms. But prediabetes ups your risk for heart disease, stroke, and type 2 diabetes.

Type 2 diabetes

If your A1c is 6.5% or higher, you have diabetes. You may have symptoms like increased thirst, blurred vision, and numbness in feet or hands. Or you may not have any symptoms at all.

Causes and Risk Factors of Type 2 Diabetes

Type 2 diabetes is mainly the result of two problems:

• Cells in muscle, fat and the liver become resistant to insulin As a result, the cells don't take in enough sugar.

• The pancreas can't make enough insulin to keep blood sugar levels within a healthy range.

Exactly why this happens is not known. Being overweight and inactive are key contributing factors.

Risk factors

Factors that may increase the risk of type 2 diabetes include:

• **Weight**. Being overweight or obese is a main risk.

• **Fat distribution**. Storing fat mainly in the abdomen — rather than the hips and thighs — indicates a greater risk. The risk of type 2 diabetes is higher in men with a waist circumference above 40 inches (101.6 centimeters) and in women with a waist measurement above 35 inches (88.9 centimeters).

• **Inactivity.** The less active a person is, the greater the risk. Physical activity helps control weight, uses up glucose as energy and makes cells more sensitive to insulin.

• **Family history.** An individual's risk of type 2 diabetes increases if a parent or sibling has type 2 diabetes.

• **Race and ethnicity.** Although it's unclear why, people of certain races and ethnicities — including Black, Hispanic, Native American and Asian people, and Pacific Islanders — are more likely to develop type 2 diabetes than white people are.

• **Blood lipid levels.** An increased risk is associated with low levels of high-density lipoprotein (HDL) cholesterol — the "good" cholesterol — and high levels of triglycerides.

- **Age**. The risk of type 2 diabetes increases with age, especially after age 35.

- **Prediabetes**. Prediabetes is a condition in which the blood sugar level is higher than normal, but not high enough to be classified as diabetes. Left untreated, prediabetes often progresses to type 2 diabetes.

- **Pregnancy-related risks**. The risk of developing type 2 diabetes is higher in people who had gestational diabetes when they were pregnant and in those who gave birth to a baby weighing more than 9 pounds (4 kilograms).

- **Polycystic ovary syndrome.** Having polycystic ovary syndrome — a condition characterized by irregular menstrual periods, excess hair growth and obesity — increases the risk of diabetes.

Symptoms and Diagnosis of Type 2 Diabetes

The early signs and symptoms of type 2 diabetes can include:

1. Frequent urination

When blood sugar levels are high, the kidneys try to remove the excess sugar by filtering it out of the blood. This can lead to a person needing to urinate more frequently, particularly at night.

2. Increased thirst

The frequent urination necessary to remove excess sugar from the blood can result in the body losing additional water. Over time, this can cause dehydration and make a person feel more thirsty than usual.

3. Frequent hunger

People with diabetes often do not get enough energy from their food.

The digestive system breaks food down into a simple sugar called glucose, which the body uses as fuel. In people with diabetes, not enough of this glucose moves from the bloodstream into the body's cells.

As a result, people with type 2 diabetes often feel constantly hungry, regardless of how recently they have eaten.

4. Fatigue

Type 2 diabetes can impact a person's energy levels and cause them to feel fatigued.

Diabetes fatigue occurs due to insufficient sugar moving from the bloodstream into the body's cells.

5. Blurry vision

An excess of sugar in the blood can damage the tiny blood vessels in the eyes, which can cause blurry vision. This can occur in one or both eyes.

High blood sugar levels can also lead to swelling of the eye lens. This can cause blurred vision but will improve when blood sugar levels reduce.

If a person with diabetes goes without treatment, the damage to these blood vessels can become more severe, and permanent vision loss may eventually occur.

6. Slow healing of cuts and wounds

High sugar levels in the blood can damage the body's nerves and blood vessels, which can impair blood circulation. As a result, even small cuts and wounds may take weeks or months to heal. Slow wound healing also increases the risk of infection.

7. Tingling, numbness, or pain in the hands or feet

High blood sugar levels can affect blood circulation and damage the nerves. In people with type 2 diabetes, this can lead to pain or a sensation of tingling or numbness in the hands and feet.

This condition is known as neuropathy. It can worsen over time and lead to more serious complications if a person does not get treatment for their diabetes.

8. Patches of darker skin

Patches of darker skin forming on creases of the neck, armpit, or groin can also result from diabetes. These patches may feel soft and velvety.

This skin condition is known as acanthosis nigricans.

9. Itching and yeast infections

Excess sugar in the blood and urine provides food for yeast, which can lead to infection. Yeast infections tend to occur on warm, moist areas of the skin, such as the mouth, genital areas, and armpits.

The affected areas are usually itchy, but a person may also experience burning, skin discoloration, and soreness.

Diagnosis

Type 2 diabetes is usually diagnosed using the glycated hemoglobin (A1C) test. This blood test indicates your average blood sugar level for the past two to three months. Results are interpreted as follows:

• Below 5.7% is normal.

• 5.7% to 6.4% is diagnosed as prediabetes.

• 6.5% or higher on two separate tests indicates diabetes.

If the A1C test isn't available, or if you have certain conditions that interfere with an A1C test, your health care provider may use the following tests to diagnose diabetes:

Random blood sugar test. Blood sugar values are expressed in milligrams of sugar per deciliter (mg/dL) or millimoles of sugar per liter (mmol/L) of blood. Regardless of when you last ate, a level of 200 mg/dL (11.1 mmol/L) or higher suggests diabetes, especially if you also have symptoms of diabetes, such as frequent urination and extreme thirst.

Fasting blood sugar test. A blood sample is taken after you haven't eaten overnight. Results are interpreted as follows:

• Less than 100 mg/dL (5.6 mmol/L) is considered healthy.

• 100 to 125 mg/dL (5.6 to 6.9 mmol/L) is diagnosed as prediabetes.

• 126 mg/dL (7 mmol/L) or higher on two separate tests is diagnosed as diabetes.

Oral glucose tolerance test. This test is less commonly used than the others, except during pregnancy. You'll need to not eat for a certain amount of time and then drink a sugary liquid at your health care provider's office. Blood sugar levels then are tested periodically for two hours. Results are interpreted as follows:

• Less than 140 mg/dL (7.8 mmol/L) after two hours is considered healthy.

• 140 to 199 mg/dL (7.8 mmol/L and 11.0 mmol/L) is diagnosed as prediabetes.

• 200 mg/dL (11.1 mmol/L) or higher after two hours suggests diabetes.

Screening. The American Diabetes Association recommends routine screening with diagnostic tests for type 2 diabetes in all adults age 35 or older and in the following groups:

• People younger than 35 who are overweight or obese and have one or more risk factors associated with diabetes.

• Women who have had gestational diabetes.

• People who have been diagnosed with prediabetes.

• Children who are overweight or obese and who have a family history of type 2 diabetes or other risk factors.

Complications of Type 2 Diabetes

Type 2 diabetes affects many major organs, including the heart, blood vessels, nerves, eyes and kidneys. Also, factors that increase the risk of diabetes are risk factors for other serious diseases. Managing diabetes and controlling blood sugar can lower the risk for these complications and other medical conditions, including:

• **Heart and blood vessel disease**. Diabetes is associated with an increased risk of heart disease, stroke, high blood pressure and narrowing of blood vessels, a condition called atherosclerosis.

• **Nerve damage in limbs.** This condition is called neuropathy. High blood sugar over time can damage or destroy nerves. That may result in tingling, numbness, burning, pain or eventual loss of feeling that usually begins at the tips of the toes or fingers and gradually spreads upward.

• **Other nerve damage.** Damage to nerves of the heart can contribute to irregular heart rhythms. Nerve damage in the digestive system can cause problems with nausea, vomiting, diarrhea or constipation. Nerve damage also may cause erectile dysfunction.

• **Kidney disease.** Diabetes may lead to chronic kidney disease or end-stage kidney disease that can't be reversed. That may require dialysis or a kidney transplant.

• **Eye damage**. Diabetes increases the risk of serious eye diseases, such as cataracts and glaucoma, and may damage the blood vessels of the retina, potentially leading to blindness.

• **Skin conditions.** Diabetes may raise the risk of some skin problems, including bacterial and fungal infections.

• **Slow healing.** Left untreated, cuts and blisters can become serious infections, which may heal poorly. Severe damage might require toe, foot or leg amputation.

• **Hearing impairment**. Hearing problems are more common in people with diabetes.

- **Sleep apnea**. Obstructive sleep apnea is common in people living with type 2 diabetes. Obesity may be the main contributing factor to both conditions.

- **Dementia**. Type 2 diabetes seems to increase the risk of Alzheimer's disease and other disorders that cause dementia. Poor control of blood sugar is linked to a more rapid decline in memory and other thinking skills.

Treatment Strategies of Type 2 Diabetes

Management of type 2 diabetes includes:

Healthy eating.

Regular exercise.

Weight loss.

Possibly, diabetes medication or insulin therapy.

Blood sugar monitoring.

These steps make it more likely that blood sugar will stay in a healthy range. And they may help to delay or prevent complications.

Healthy eating

There's no specific diabetes diet. However, it's important to center your diet around:

A regular schedule for meals and healthy snacks.

Smaller portion sizes.

More high-fiber foods, such as fruits, nonstarchy vegetables and whole grains.

Fewer refined grains, starchy vegetables and sweets.

Modest servings of low-fat dairy, low-fat meats and fish.

Healthy cooking oils, such as olive oil or canola oil.

Fewer calories.

Your health care provider may recommend seeing a registered dietitian, who can help you:

Identify healthy food choices.

Plan well-balanced, nutritional meals.

Develop new habits and address barriers to changing habits.

Monitor carbohydrate intake to keep your blood sugar levels more stable.

Physical activity

Exercise is important for losing weight or maintaining a healthy weight. It also helps with managing blood sugar. Talk to your health care provider before starting or changing your exercise program to ensure that activities are safe for you.

Aerobic exercise. Choose an aerobic exercise that you enjoy, such as walking, swimming, biking or running. Adults should aim for 30 minutes or more of moderate aerobic exercise on most days of the week, or at least 150 minutes a week.

Resistance exercise. Resistance exercise increases your strength, balance and ability to perform activities of daily living more easily. Resistance training includes weightlifting, yoga and calisthenics. Adults living with type 2 diabetes should aim for 2 to 3 sessions of resistance exercise each week.

Limit inactivity. Breaking up long periods of inactivity, such as sitting at the computer, can help control blood sugar levels. Take a few minutes to stand, walk around or do some light activity every 30 minutes.

Weight loss

Weight loss results in better control of blood sugar levels, cholesterol, triglycerides and blood pressure. If you're overweight, you may begin to see improvements in these factors after losing as little as 5% of your body weight. However, the more weight you lose, the greater the benefit to your health. In some cases, losing up to 15% of body weight may be recommended.

Your health care provider or dietitian can help you set appropriate weight-loss goals and encourage lifestyle changes to help you achieve them.

Monitoring your blood sugar

Your health care provider will advise you on how often to check your blood sugar level to make sure you remain within your target range. You may, for example, need to check it once a day and before or after exercise. If you take insulin, you may need to check your blood sugar multiple times a day.

Monitoring is usually done with a small, at-home device called a blood glucose meter, which measures the amount of sugar in a drop of blood. Keep a record of your measurements to share with your health care team.

Continuous glucose monitoring is an electronic system that records glucose levels every few minutes from a sensor placed under the skin. Information can be transmitted to a mobile device such as a phone, and the system can send alerts when levels are too high or too low.

Diabetes medications

If you can't maintain your target blood sugar level with diet and exercise, your health care provider may prescribe diabetes medications that help lower glucose levels, or your provider may suggest insulin therapy. Medicines for type 2 diabetes include the following.

Metformin (Fortamet, Glumetza, others) is generally the first medicine prescribed for type 2 diabetes. It works mainly by lowering glucose production in the liver and improving the body's sensitivity to insulin so it uses insulin more effectively.

Some people experience B-12 deficiency and may need to take supplements. Other possible side effects, which may improve over time, include:

- Nausea.
- Abdominal pain.
- Bloating.
- Diarrhea.

Sulfonylureas help the body secrete more insulin. Examples include glyburide (DiaBeta, Glynase), glipizide (Glucotrol XL) and glimepiride (Amaryl). Possible side effects include:

- Low blood sugar.
- Weight gain.

Glinides stimulate the pancreas to secrete more insulin. They're faster acting than sulfonylureas. But their effect in the body is shorter. Examples include repaglinide and nateglinide. Possible side effects include:

- Low blood sugar.
- Weight gain.

Thiazolidinediones make the body's tissues more sensitive to insulin. An example of this medicine is pioglitazone (Actos). Possible side effects include:

- Risk of congestive heart failure.

- Risk of bladder cancer (pioglitazone).

- Risk of bone fractures.

- Weight gain.

DPP-4 inhibitors help reduce blood sugar levels but tend to have a very modest effect. Examples include sitagliptin (Januvia), saxagliptin (Onglyza) and linagliptin (Tradjenta). Possible side effects include:

- Risk of pancreatitis.
- Joint pain.

GLP-1 receptor agonists are injectable medications that slow digestion and help lower blood sugar levels. Their use is often associated with weight loss, and some may reduce the risk of heart attack and stroke. Examples include exenatide (Byetta, Bydureon Bcise), liraglutide (Saxenda, Victoza) and semaglutide (Rybelsus, Ozempic, Wegovy). Possible side effects include:

- Risk of pancreatitis.
- Nausea.
- Vomiting.
- Diarrhea.

SGLT2 inhibitors affect the blood-filtering functions in the kidneys by blocking the return of glucose to the bloodstream. As a result, glucose is removed in the urine. These medicines may reduce the risk of heart attack and stroke in people with a high risk of those conditions. Examples include canagliflozin (Invokana), dapagliflozin (Farxiga) and empagliflozin (Jardiance). Possible side effects include:

- Vaginal yeast infections.

- Urinary tract infections.

- Low blood pressure.

- High cholesterol.

- Risk of gangrene.

- Risk of bone fractures (canagliflozin).

- Risk of amputation (canagliflozin).

Other medicines your health care provider might prescribe in addition to diabetes medications include blood pressure and cholesterol-lowering medicines, as well as low-dose aspirin, to help prevent heart and blood vessel disease.

Insulin therapy

Some people who have type 2 diabetes need insulin therapy. In the past, insulin therapy was used as a last resort, but today it may be prescribed sooner if blood sugar targets aren't met with lifestyle changes and other medicines.

Different types of insulin vary on how quickly they begin to work and how long they have an effect. Long-acting insulin, for example, is designed to work overnight or throughout the day to keep blood sugar levels stable. Short-acting insulin generally is used at mealtime.

Your health care provider will determine what type of insulin is right for you and when you should take it. Your insulin type, dosage and schedule may change depending on how stable your blood sugar levels are. Most types of insulin are taken by injection.

Side effects of insulin include the risk of low blood sugar — a condition called hypoglycemia — diabetic ketoacidosis and high triglycerides.

Weight-loss surgery

Weight-loss surgery changes the shape and function of the digestive system. This surgery may help you lose weight and manage type 2 diabetes and other conditions related to obesity. There are several surgical procedures. All of them help people lose weight by limiting how much food they can eat. Some procedures also limit the amount of nutrients the body can absorb.

Weight-loss surgery is only one part of an overall treatment plan. Treatment also includes diet and nutritional supplement guidelines, exercise and mental health care.

Generally, weight-loss surgery may be an option for adults living with type 2 diabetes who have a body mass index (BMI) of 35 or higher. BMI is a formula that uses weight and height to estimate body fat. Depending on the severity of diabetes or the presence of other medical conditions, surgery may be an option for someone with a BMI lower than 35.

Weight-loss surgery requires a lifelong commitment to lifestyle changes. Long-term side effects may include nutritional deficiencies and osteoporosis.

Chapter 2: Introduction to Canning for Diabetes

S ince the beginning of time, people have needed to preserve food. The process could take considerable time and energy, but it was better than going hungry in the winter. Early methods of preservation included smoking, drying, fermenting, or cooling/freezing foods (given the right type of environment). Later, more methods were developed such as pickling in an acid (such as vinegar), curing with salts, and making jams or jellies with honey and sugar. None of these approaches were ideal and the search continued for better methods that were quicker, more reliable, and made the food easy to store and transport.

From our modern perspective we can also see that several of these approaches tend to be unhealthy. Either the process itself causes harm to the food (i.e. the smoking process generates carcinogens), or the process involves adding enormous amounts of unhealthy compounds, such as salt and sugar. Those interested in preserving food for health reasons will find many older methods wanting.

In the late 1700's Napoleon Bonaparte catalyzed the search for a better method of food preservation. He believed that, "An army travels on its stomach," and was looking for a better way to feed his armies. Accordingly, Napoleon offered a fortune to anyone who developed a method of preserving food on a large scale. Nicholas Appert claimed the prize years later in 1810, but it still took around 50 years before his method trickled down to the average family. This occurred soon after 1858, when John Mason invented the iconic, reusable "Mason Jar".

Canning became extremely popular. It was a safe, effective, inexpensive, and relatively simple process. People were now able to use one method to preserve just about anything: fruits, vegetables, soups, sauces, and meats.

The canning process is quite simple. First, a tin can or glass jar is filled with food and liquid (usually water). After the container has been sealed, it is heated and often put under pressure. This process kills any microorganisms that could cause illness or spoil food. When the can or jar is removed from the water, the air inside compresses and seals the contents off from the outside world. The seal then protects the food from new microorganisms entering and from oxidization from the air. After this, the food can be conveniently stored and enjoyed at a later date.

There are two main types of canning methods:

Water bath canning (Also known as "Hot Water Canning" or "Boiling Water Bath.") – Water-bath canning is only for produce that is HIGH in acid. Such as for tomatoes, berries, and making pickles. It helps preserve the food without the use of high pressure. Will need a large pot.

Pressure canning – Pressure canning is the only safe method of preserving low-acid foods at high temperatures. Low-acid foods include vegetables, meats, beans, and soup. Will need a pressure canner and canning kit equipment.

Until the arrival of our modern grocery stores, canning remained common in nearly every household. It was a necessity and a way of life. Contrast this with today. Only a couple generations have passed and the art of food preservation has been lost to the vast majority of people. However, interest in food preservation has been growing over the past few years and canning, in particular, is seeing a resurgence of popularity. There are many reasons for this:

Save money – Hey, food can be expensive. Buying or picking foods in season and canning them for future use can save you some extra money. This is especially true when you consider the quality of the foods you are getting. You may be surprised how gourmet your home canned food can taste.

Preserve harvest – This is something gardeners will understand. You wait patiently for a few months until your garden to start producing, then you are suddenly swamped with far more produce than you are prepared to deal with. Sure, you can give some to family, friends, or neighbors, but you'll still have more. Canning the extras is a sensible way to avoid waste and enjoy your produce year-round.

Prepare for bad economic times – Many people are worried about the times that we live in. If something happens to our economy or our ability to affordably purchase food, people want to be prepared. Learning to can is just one of the steps people tend to take—if you ask us, it is a lot more practical than a bomb shelter.

Eco friendly – Canning your own food is an excellent way to reduce your environmental impact. Especially if the food is home grown, you remove the countless miles food is shipped from the farm, to the factory, and then to the distributor and local store. You also reduce packaging waste because canning jars (except for the lids) are reusable and will last for years.

Sentimental connection/ gifts – Many people enjoy canning because it reminds them of a simpler time. Perhaps it was an activity that their mother or grandmother used to do. Additionally, canned foods make great gifts. The work and care that went into a homemade jam or homemade pickles is worth much more than the food itself.

Quality taste – It's a fact, homemade food simply tastes better. You can't beat a quality home-canned product made from fresh, locally grown ingredients. In the store, you could easily pay double for such a product. Even if your initial investment fails to save you money (due to buying jars, a canner, etc.), you'll have a healthier, tastier product stocked in your pantry. Another benefit is that you'll be able to tweak recipes to your exact tastes and even experiment with new flavor combinations.

Health – While canning is not the absolute healthiest method of food preservation (e.g. freezing preserves more nutrients), it does have many benefits. Because you canned it yourself, you will know exactly what you are eating. You can be assured that the food was fresh and high quality. You will also be enjoying food that is free from harmful additives and preservatives.

Chapter 3: Essential Canning Equipment and Techniques

Now that you are sold on the benefits of canning, and are sure it can be done safely, you are ready to get started. But wait, do you have everything you need? Is the box of canning supplies in your basement complete?

Here is a list of all the supplies you need to can, plus a few extras that are extremely helpful:

1. Jars and lids

The first thing you will need to get is canning jars. In America, common brands include Ball and Kerr, but any brand will do. Jars in other parts of the world may be different, but will work in a similar manner. Look for solidly built, wide mouth jars. Be aware that jars come in different sizes. Half pint, pint, and quart are the most common. Different sizes tend to be used for different types of recipes, i.e. pint jars are common for jams and quarts are common for pickles or soups.

Most canning lids contain two parts: screw bands and flat lids that have a built-in gasket. The screw bands can actually be removed for storage after the canning is complete (this helps prevent rusting during storage). Then, they can be used again in the future. Although some people reuse their lids, we recommend against it. They are cheap and the risk of a seal failing (and spoiling your food or making you sick) outweighs any money you may save by reusing gaskets. However, if a jar does fail to seal, don't throw it away- you can put it in the refrigerator and eat it first.

For people who want to reuse their lids from year to year, we recommend purchasing reusable canning lids. These lids actually come with separate rubber gasket rings rather than a thin attached gasket. They will cost roughly two to three times more than regular lids, but you can start saving money after a few years.

2. Water bath or pressure canner

Water bath canning can be done in any large pot, as long as the jars fit and can be submerged in water. However, you will also need to add a canning rack to the bottom of the pot. This is to keep the jars off of the bottom of the canner and allow the water to completely surround the jars and evenly heat the food inside.

You can also buy water bath canners that have been specifically designed to accommodate jars and a canning rack. Some are even sold as canning kits, which include other useful tools such as a jar lifter and wide mouth funnel (we will discuss these in detail below).

If you are planning on canning low acid foods you will need to invest in a pressure canner. A pressure canner is different from a pressure cooker. Most pressure cookers are not safe for canning use. If you can use your pressure cooker for canning, the instruction manual will say so. Pressure cookers are often too small for canning anyway.

The great thing about a pressure canner—besides being able to can low acid foods—is that it can also be used as a water bath canner or a pressure cooker. It is a piece of cookware that gives you a lot of options.

3. Canning utensils

You could probably get by without these tools, but they are strongly recommended. They will make your canning much easier and safer. The tools themselves are cheap; if you don't invest in them, expect to pay with burnt fingers and broken or poorly sealed jars. Each utensil can be bought separately, but it is usually cheaper to buy them as part of a home canning kit.

• **Jar lifter**—This is a large tongs that is designed for lifting jars in or out of boiling water.

Remember, the jars can be quite heavy; using tongs that are designed for something else is a sure way to hurt yourself or break something.

• **Magnetic lid lifter**—Essentially a magnet on a stick. Sometimes it is called a lid wand. It is used to pluck canning lids out of boiling water (where they are sterilized). You could pick them up with tongs, but the lid lifter makes it easier to seat the lids on the jar without contaminating them.

• **Wide mouth canning funnel**—This kind of funnel will make filling your jars so much easier. Also, the funnel will help keep your counters, and more importantly, the lips of your jars clean (so they seal properly).

• **Bubble freer**—This is a simple instrument that normally comes with canning kits. It is used when canning to pop any large bubbles that form inside the jar when you fill it with food. You could just as easily use a butter knife or a skewer.

• **A stack of kitchen towels**—these won't be included in your canning kit, but you probably have a bunch of them already. Cotton towels that are easy to wash work best (they will get dirty). Use them as hot pads or to wipe up spills and drips. Lay some out on your counters to catch spills and insulate the counter surface. Some counter surfaces (especially granite or tile) tend to be cold and can actually cause a hot jar to crack due to temperature differences—the towels help prevent this.

4. Good canning book, information, processing times, recipes

A good canning book will give you some fail-safe recipes and a detailed explanation of canning methods and processes.

Before you start canning you will want to have your recipe picked out and ready to reference. You should also have looked up the processing time, as it varies by altitude and food type. It's no fun to go rummaging through the cupboards when things are boiling over.

5. Thickening agents

Although these are technically ingredients, we felt like listing them here because they are a common element of many recipes. However, many people do not realize they are required until they start looking at recipes. Both are used to thicken or gel the liquid in your recipe. Recipes that do not require thickening agents will simply leave these ingredients out.

Cornstarch is often used to thicken the liquid in cans. However, cornstarch tends to break down after it has been heated. It also does not thicken high acid solutions well. Clear Jel is the answer to these problems. It is a modified cornstarch that is excellent for canning. Unlike normal cornstarch, Clear Jel retains its thickening powers after it has been heated and also works in acidic environments. If you compare a can that contains regular cornstarch with a can that contains Clear Jel, you will see a clear difference in thickness and consistency.

Pectin is a naturally occurring heteropolysaccharide found in the cell walls of plants. It is found in particularly high amounts in apples and citrus plants (which is where the pectin you buy at a store is sourced). Pectin is used to set (or gel) fruit and fruit juices and make them spreadable. Pectin also allows you to use less sugar than other recipes (sugar also helps jams set). Several manufacturers make pectins for full or low sugar recipes. Low-ester pectins (also called low methoxyl pectins) use calcium ions in water to form gel and therefore require less sugar.

6. Quality food

Of course nobody is planning on canning marbles or erasers, food is the most important part. We only mention this obvious fact to say that food quality matters. In canning, make it your goal to use the freshest ingredients possible. This will not only improve the way your foods look and taste, but their nutritional content as well.

Try to get foods from your local farmers' markets, or grow them in your home garden. Besides the food quality, you will learn more about food production and become more connected with nature.

How to Choose Diabetes-Friendly Ingredients

Food choices are a key part of managing diabetes. Eating fewer carbohydrates, limiting highly processed foods, and choosing more natural food options can help you manage your blood sugar.

When you have diabetes, your body has difficulty using the glucose (sugar) that comes from the food you eat. As of 2023, the Centers for Disease Control and Prevention (CDC) estimates that over 38.4

million people in the United States have diabetes. Most of those people have type 2 diabetes.

If glucose levels are consistently above your target range, it can lead to health complications. Common health complications include:

• Kidney disease, which can lead to kidney failure

• Nerve and blood vessel disease, which can lead to limb amputation

• Eye disease, which can lead to blindness

Weight loss and exercise have shown enormous potential for preventing and treating type 2 diabetes. In some cases, they have even put type 2 diabetes in remission.

Maintaining a diabetes-friendly diet is more complex than just cutting carbs. Don't let that deter you, though. It can be pretty easy to follow a diabetes-friendly diet, especially if you get into the habit of meal planning.

Planning your meals ahead of time

Planning your meals might take a little bit of time, but you'll reap the rewards later. If you've already decided what you're making each night of the week and have your refrigerator stocked, you're that much closer to a healthy meal.

Getting into a routine of meal planning makes staying on track with a healthy eating plan easier. It's especially useful on days when life gets busy or stressful.

All it takes is a one-day commitment to get on the right path, said Toby Smithson, MSNW, RDN, LDN, CDE, co-author of Diabetes Meal Planning and Nutrition for Dummies and a former spokesperson for the Academy of Nutrition and Dietetics.

She suggested following these tips:

• Pick one day per week where you can set aside a couple of hours for meal planning. This could be a weekend day or another non-working day. If you have children, look for a day when you don't have to transport them around for various activities.

• To get started, write a menu for the week. Scour Pinterest or your favorite food blogs for ideas, and write down a shopping list as you go. Then hit the grocery store using your list as a guide.

• If you want to make this process even quicker, consider using a meal-planning website such as Plan to Eat. Websites and apps like this allow you to quickly save and categorize recipes from any website, blog, cookbook, or meal plan. Plan to Eat also automatically creates a grocery list for you.

• After you've done this for several weeks, you'll have a great database of recipes you enjoy. It'll become easier to make your plan because you'll be able to spend less time finding recipes. And, of course, you can always add new recipes as you come across them, so you don't get bored.

• If cooking daily isn't feasible for you, give yourself a break. Try cooking in bulk when you can. You can also look for meals that are easy to freeze and reheat later.

As you put together your meal plans for the week, follow these tips to find the best foods for you that are both tasty and diabetes-friendly.

Fruits and vegetables

Here's your chance to go wild! Every fruit and vegetable has its own set of nutrients and health benefits.

Try to choose fruits and vegetables in a range of colors, and include some in every meal or snack.

Non-starchy vegetables are the lowest in calories and carbohydrates, so they're a great choice for people with diabetes. Some options include:

• Broccoli

• Cauliflower

- Brussels sprouts

- Green beans

- Eggplant

- Asparagus

- Celery

- Salad greens

- Carrots

- Zucchini

You'll need to count the carbs in your fruits and starchy vegetables just as you would for any other carbohydrate food group. This doesn't mean you need to avoid them — just be sure the amount you're eating fits into your overall meal plan.

Shelley Wishnick, a registered dietitian and diabetes clinical manager at the medical equipment company Medtronic, recommended that people with diabetes stick to 1 serving of fruit per meal. Grab half a banana, a fruit the size of your fist, or half a cup of chopped fruit.

When shopping for fruits and vegetables, look for choices that are in season to save some money. Frozen produce is also a budget-friendly option that's convenient for busy mornings or weeknights.

Meat and seafood

Choose fatty fish for heart health and brain protection. Seafood that contains omega-3 fatty acids, such as salmon or canned tuna, is a great option. This is because omega-3 fatty acids support a healthy heart. Other options for fish may include trout, catfish, and cod.

Try to get at least 2 servings of fish per week.

When it comes to meat, stick with options like:

• Chicken

• Turkey breast

• Lean cuts of pork

• Lean cuts of beef

Aim to fit 1 or 2 servings of lean meat per day into your meal plan.

Registered dietitian **Jill Weisenberger**, author of **The Overworked Person's Guide to Better Nutrition**, advised against bacon and sausages.

These foods don't offer a lot of protein and can be high in sodium and fat.

You may want to consider limiting your red meats and processed meat. They've been linked to colon cancer, a condition you're at a higher risk of if you have diabetes.

Legumes

The legume family includes the following foods:

- Beans

- Peanuts

- Peas

- Lentils

Aim for at least 1–2 servings per day. Although these foods are rich in carbohydrates, they're a great source of fiber and plant protein. This makes them an ideal carbohydrate choice over other starches, such as rice, white pasta, and bread.

Dairy and dairy alternatives

Some studies in a 2019 research review suggest that yogurt is good for people with diabetes and may help prevent it for those at risk of the condition. Greek yogurt is a good option because it's higher in protein and lower in carbs than traditional yogurt.

Just watch out for added sugars in yogurts. They can hide in flavorings and add-ins, such as granola or cookie bits. Overall, options that are lower in calories, added sugar, and saturated fat are better if you have diabetes.

Cottage cheese is another great low carb dairy option that's also high in protein.

Unsweetened soy milk is a nondairy milk option that's also a source of protein. Other nondairy milks — like flax, almond, or hemp milk — and yogurt made from them often contain little or no protein. Learn more about nondairy milks.

Frozen foods

You can stock up on fruits and veggies, too! Read the nutrient label to avoid products with lots of additives, sugar, or sodium. When choosing frozen vegetables, opt for plain vegetables instead of ones with sauces.

These are always handy to keep stocked because frozen produce lasts longer than fresh produce and can be great for saving time when you're pulling together dinner in a pinch.

Frozen fish and shrimp are other good choices. They're quick to cook and keep longer than fresh versions, said Weisenberger. She likes these for pulling together a wholesome meal on a busy day.

When you're hankering for something sweet, there's no need to ditch dessert altogether. Restrictive diets aren't a good long-term solution and can often do more harm than good.

Instead, be smart about what you eat. Stick to single-serving desserts and stock your freezer with only one type at a time. This can help you avoid eating more than an intended serving.

Breakfast cereals and snacks

It's best to limit processed foods when you can, but that's not always possible. Whether it's breakfast cereal, crackers, or snack bars, certain keywords can help you find options that are better for you. In general, check the packaging for these words:

• Whole Grain

• Whole Wheat

• Sprouted Grain

• High Fiber

Instead of buying a lot of processed snack foods, consider reaching for some nuts. In addition to heart health benefits, some nuts, such as almonds, may even help increase insulin sensitivity — a good thing for people with diabetes.

Grains

Eating too many carbs can cause blood sugar spikes, so try to take care when choosing grains. It helps to read labels for serving sizes and total carbohydrates, as it's easy to overeat these foods.

When possible, **choose whole grains.** These are higher in fiber, protein, and other nutrients, so they'll keep you fuller for longer. Some options include:

• Corn

• Oats

• Buckwheat

• Quinoa

You might find that baked goods and products made from flour, even whole wheat flour, cause your blood sugar to spike. If this is the case for you, look for whole grains that are minimally processed, naturally higher in fiber, and in their whole food form.

Pairing these intact whole grains with healthy fats or protein can help reduce blood sugar rises.

Canned goods

Canned fruits and vegetables are other good choices when fresh produce isn't available. As with frozen foods, it's important to watch out for added sugars and sodium. Choose fruits canned in juice, not syrup, and look for low sodium vegetables.

Chapter 4: Fruit Preserves and Spreads

Intense Strawberry Preserves

Ingredients

• 4 pounds fresh strawberries, washed and patted dry

• Honey

• ⅓ cup fresh lemon juice

Directions

1. Before starting the recipe, gather the needed equipment (see Equipment tips below).

2. Hull strawberries and cut any large ones in half. Combine with lemon juice in a large, nonreactive

bowl (see Tips). Cover and let stand for 4 hours at room temperature or refrigerate overnight.

3. When you are ready to cook, prepare 5 half-pint (1-cup) jars and lids: Wash in hot soapy water and rinse well. Place the rack in the pot and place the jars, right side up, on the rack. Add enough water to fill and cover the jars by at least 1 inch. Cover the pot and bring to a boil; boil, covered, for 10 minutes, then turn off the heat. Keep the jars in the hot water (with the pot covered) while you prepare the recipe.

4. Meanwhile, place the new lids in a small saucepan, cover with water and bring to a gentle simmer. Very gently simmer for 10 minutes (taking care not to boil). Turn off the heat and keep the lids in the water until ready to use.

5. Place a saucer and 4 small spoons in the freezer for testing the consistency of the preserves later.

6. Stir the strawberries to evenly distribute the honey and transfer to a heavy 6- to 8-quart nonreactive pot. Place over medium heat and cook, stirring frequently, until the sugar has melted completely and the strawberries begin to foam, 5 to 15 minutes.

7. Increase the heat to high and boil rapidly, stirring frequently and scraping the bottom with a heatproof spatula to prevent sticking, until the mixture looks thick, shiny and darker, 15 to 20 minutes. If the jam begins to boil close to the top of the pot or scorch on the bottom, immediately reduce the heat.

8. To test if the preserves are ready, remove from heat and place a little of the preserve liquid on one of the spoons from the freezer. Rest it on the saucer and return to the freezer for 3 to 4 minutes. Drop the sample from the spoon onto the saucer: If it's thick enough to stay mounded without running or spreading, the preserves are ready. If it's too runny, return the pot to a boil and cook for about 5 minutes before testing again. When the preserves are done, skim excess foam from the surface.

9. Remove the sterilized jars from the water and place on a clean towel (if they're placed on a cold surface, the jars could crack). Using a funnel, fill jars to within 1/4 inch of the rim. (Any extra preserves can be stored in a small container in the refrigerator.) Run a chopstick around the inside of the jar to release air bubbles. Wipe the rim with a

clean cloth. Use a lid wand (or tongs) to remove the lids from the hot water. Place lids and dry rings on the jars. Tighten until just finger-tight (won't move with gentle pressure) but don't overtighten.

10. To process the filled jars: Using a jar lifter, return jars to the pot with the warm water, placing them on the rack without touching one another or the sides of the pot. If the water does not cover the jars by 1 to 2 inches, add boiling water as needed. Cover the pot and bring to a boil; boil 5 minutes, then turn off the heat, uncover the pot and leave the jars in the water for 5 minutes. Use the jar lifter to transfer the jars to a towel, with some space between each jar. Let stand, without moving, for 24 hours. (If you do not want to process the jars in a boiling-water bath, you can refrigerate the preserves for up to 2 months.)

11. After 24 hours, unscrew the rings and test the seals by pressing lightly on the center of each lid. They should have a slight concave indentation and neither yield to your pressure nor pop back. If a seal is not complete, you can process again in boiling water or store any unsealed jars in the refrigerator.

Equipment

5 half-pint (1-cup) canning jars, canning equipment

Fresh Fruit Butter

Ingredients

• 6 cups prepared fresh fruit, peeled if desired (see Tip)

- 1 cup water

- 1/2-1 cup granulated sugar , or brown sugar (honey can be used in place of sugar)

- 1 tablespoon freshly grated lemon, lime or orange zest , (optional)

- 1/4 cup lemon, lime or orange juice , (optional)

Directions

1. Combine fruit, water and honey to taste in a Dutch oven; add citrus zest and juice if using. Bring to a boil over high heat. Reduce heat to maintain a lively simmer and cook, mashing the fruit and stirring occasionally at first and then often as it thickens, until the mixture is very thick, 20 minutes to 1 hour (depending on the type of fruit). To test doneness, put a spoonful of fruit

butter on a plate. If no liquid seeps from the edges, it's done. Return to a simmer to thicken more if necessary. For very smooth fruit butter, puree in a food processor or blender, then strain and push the mixture through a sieve before storing.

2. If freezing or refrigerating, ladle the fruit butter into clean canning jars to within 1/2 inch of the rim. Wipe rims clean. Cover with lids. Let the jars stand at room temperature until cool before refrigerating or freezing. Or process in a water bath to store at room temperature (see Tip).

Tips

Make Ahead Tip: Store in the refrigerator for up to 3 weeks, in the freezer for up to 1 year or at room temperature for up to 1 year if processed in a water bath.

Equipment: Two 8-ounce canning jars

Tip: How to Prep & Measure Fruit--Berries: Remove stems; hull strawberries. Measure whole. Cherries: Remove stems and pits; halve. Measure halves. Peaches, Nectarines & Plums: Peel if desired. Cut into 1/2-inch pieces; discard pits. Measure pieces. Apples, Pears & other fruit: Peel if desired. Quarter, remove seeds and cut into 1/2-inch pieces. Measure pieces.

To peel stone fruit, dip them in boiling water for about 1 minute to loosen their skins. Let cool slightly, then remove the skins with a paring knife.

Note: 3/4 cup maple syrup (or honey) or 1/2-1 cup Splenda Granular can be used in place of 1 cup sugar.

Fresh Fruit Chutney

Ingredients

• 1 tablespoon canola oil

• 4 cups chopped onion

• 1 tablespoon minced garlic

• 8 cups prepared fresh fruit, peeled if desired (see Tip)

• 1 cup dried fruit, chopped if larger than raisins

• 1 cup granulated sugar , or brown sugar (Honey can be used in place of sugar)

• 1 cup vinegar

• 1 cup water

- 2 small fresh chile peppers, seeded and slivered lengthwise, or 1 teaspoon crushed red pepper

- 1 teaspoon salt

Directions

1. Heat oil in a Dutch oven over medium heat. Add onion and cook, stirring occasionally, until light brown, 6 to 10 minutes Add garlic and cook, stirring, until fragrant, about 30 seconds.

2. Add fresh fruit, dried fruit, sugar, vinegar, water, chiles and salt. Bring to a boil over high heat, stirring often. Reduce heat to maintain a lively simmer and cook until thickened, 30 to 40 minutes. To test doneness, put a spoonful of chutney on a plate and draw a spoon through the

center. If no liquid seeps into the middle, it's done. Return to a simmer to thicken more if necessary.

3. If freezing or refrigerating, ladle the chutney into clean canning jars to within 1/2 inch of the rim. Wipe rims clean. Cover with lids. Let the jars stand at room temperature until cool before refrigerating or freezing. Or process in a water bath to store at room temperature (see Tip).

Tips

Make Ahead Tip: Store in the refrigerator for up to 3 weeks, in the freezer for up to 1 year or at room temperature for up to 1 year if processed in a water bath.

Equipment: Six 8-ounce canning jars

Tip: How to Prep & Measure Fruit--Berries: Remove stems; hull strawberries. Measure whole. Cherries: Remove stems and pits; halve. Measure halves. Peaches, Nectarines & Plums: Peel if desired. Cut into 1/2-inch pieces; discard pits. Measure pieces. Apples, Pears & other fruit: Peel if desired. Quarter, remove seeds and cut into 1/2-inch pieces. Measure pieces.

To peel stone fruit, dip them in boiling water for about 1 minute to loosen their skins. Let cool slightly, then remove the skins with a paring knife.

Note: 3/4 cup maple syrup (or honey) or 1/2-1 cup Splenda Granular can be used in place of 1 cup sugar.

Tip: Processing in a boiling water bath ensures safe storage at room temperature for up to a year.

Raspberry Vinegar Dressing

Ingredients

- 3 tablespoons raspberry vinegar

- 1 tablespoon honey

- 2 tablespoons extra-virgin olive oil

- ⅛ teaspoon salt

- Ground pepper to taste

Directions

1. Whisk vinegar and honey in a small bowl until blended. Whisking continuously, slowly add oil. Season with salt and pepper to taste. (Alternatively, combine Ingredients in a small jar, secure the lid and shake.)

Strawberry-Rhubarb Jam

Ingredients

• 2 pounds fresh strawberries, hulled and halved (6 cups)

• 3 cups chopped rhubarb, fresh or frozen (thawed)

• 2 ½ cups granulated sugar

• ¼ teaspoon salt

• 2 teaspoons lemon juice

Directions

1. Combine strawberries, rhubarb, sugar and salt in a heavy 6-quart pot; bring to a simmer over medium-high heat, stirring often. Reduce heat to

medium; simmer, stirring often, until the mixture registers 220 degrees F on a candy thermometer and becomes thick and slightly darker, about 1 1/2 hours. (Alternatively, to test for proper thickness, place a small amount of jam on a chilled plate; place in freezer for 2 minutes then run a finger over the jam. If it wrinkles and feels gel-like, the jam is ready. If the jam is not yet ready, continue cooking for 5 minutes, then test again.) Remove from heat; stir in lemon juice.

2. Spoon the jam into 2 sterilized (1-pint) jars; let cool to room temperature, about 1 hour. Cover and refrigerate for up to 1 month.

Tips

To make ahead: Refrigerate for up to 1 month.

Equipment: Candy thermometer; two 1-pint jars

Homemade Fruit Preserves

Ingredients

• 4 pounds fresh fruit, such as strawberries, blackberries, figs, watermelon, apples, pears and/or citrus, peeled, sliced and/or diced

• 4 pounds granulated sugar

• 1 lemon or lime, thinly sliced

Directions

1. Toss fruit, sugar and lemon (or lime) slices in a large pot. Cover and let macerate overnight.

2. Transfer the pot to the stove and bring the mixture to a simmer over medium heat, stirring

occasionally. Cover, lower the heat to maintain a simmer and cook until the fruit shrinks slightly and the syrup starts to turn the pale color of the fruit, adding water as needed to keep the syrup pale and thin, at least 15 minutes and up to 1 hour. (For fruits like strawberries, blackberries, figs and watermelon flesh, 15 minutes may be all the time you need. For apples, pears, citrus and watermelon rinds, you'll need to cook them a bit longer until some of the fruit becomes translucent.) Remove from heat and let cool for at least 1 hour.

3. Transfer the fruit and syrup into jars, cover tightly and refrigerate for up to 3 months.

To make ahead

Refrigerate for up to 3 months.

Green Tomato Jam

Ingredients

- 2 pounds green tomatoes, cored and chopped

- 1 ½ cups granulated sugar

- 1 teaspoon grated lemon zest

- 2 tablespoons lemon juice, divided

- ¼ teaspoon salt

Directions

1. Toss green tomatoes, sugar and 1 tablespoon lemon juice together in a large nonreactive bowl until well combined. Cover and refrigerate for at least 1 hour or up to 12 hours.

2. Transfer the tomato mixture to a large nonreactive pot and bring to a gentle boil over medium-high heat. Reduce heat to low and simmer, stirring occasionally, until the mixture bubbles, thickens and becomes syrup-like, 35 to 45 minutes. Stir in lemon zest, salt and the remaining 1 tablespoon lemon juice.

3. Working in batches, if needed, pour the tomato mixture into a blender. Secure the lid on the blender and remove the center piece to allow steam to escape. Place a clean towel over the opening. Process until mostly smooth, 10 to 15 seconds. (Use caution when pureeing hot liquids.) Transfer to a medium nonreactive bowl or a pint-size mason jar. Refrigerate, uncovered, to chill completely before serving, about 30 minutes.

Serve chilled or cover airtight and refrigerate for up to 3 weeks.

Preserved Citrus Paste

Ingredients

• 1 pound pound citrus (about 3 lemons, 5 limes, 2 oranges or 1 grapefruit), preferably organic

• ½ cup kosher salt

• Lemon, lime or grapefruit juice as needed

Directions

1. Scrub fruit, being sure to remove any stickers. Trim stem ends of lemons, limes or oranges; trim both ends of grapefruit. Cut the fruit into 1 1/2-inch-thick wedges.

2. Pack the fruit in a sterilized pint-size glass jar, layering salt between each wedge. Use a wooden spoon to press the fruit down and release the juice and make room for more fruit. Top off with enough citrus juice to cover the fruit, if needed.

3. Seal the jar tightly with the lid and leave it in a cool place, such as your countertop. Flip upside-down once or twice a day for 3 days so that the salt and juice distribute throughout the jar. You might need to open the jar and press the fruit down to keep it submerged. After a week, transfer the jar to the refrigerator for at least 2 weeks.

4. Rinse the citrus to remove excess salt. Puree in a food processor or blender. Refrigerate the paste for up to 1 year.

Raspberry Ginger Lime Seltzer

Ingredients

Fruit concentrate

- ¼ cup raspberries, fresh or frozen (thawed)

- ½ lime, sliced

- 1 teaspoon sliced fresh ginger

- 3 fresh mint leaves

- 1 cup water

Simple syrup

- 1 cup sugar or honey

- 1 cup water

Seltzer

• 3 cups seltzer water

Directions

1. To make fruit concentrate: place raspberries, lime, ginger, and mint leaves in a pitcher or large jar and smash with a wooden spoon to release their juices. Stir in water. Let the mixture infuse in the fridge overnight, then strain.

2. To make simple syrup: combine water and sugar (or honey) in a small saucepan over medium heat. Simmer, stirring occasionally, until completely dissolved. Let cool.

3. To make soda: for each serving of soda, combine 1/4 cup fruit concentrate, 1 tsp. simple syrup and

3/4 cup seltzer water in a glass. Serve with ice if desired.

Tips

To make ahead: The fruit concentrate will keep, covered, in the refrigerator for up to 3 days. The syrup will keep, covered, in the fridge for up to 1 week.

Tip: Create additional seltzer flavors using these combinations for the fruit concentrate.

Cranberry Orange Ginger:

1/2 cup cranberries, fresh or frozen (thawed)

1/2 orange, sliced

1 tsp. sliced fresh ginger

Pineapple Lemon Ginger:

1 cup chopped pineapple, fresh or frozen (thawed)

1/2 lemon, sliced

1 tsp. sliced fresh ginger

Tomato Jam

Ingredients

- 2 pounds plum tomatoes, cored and chopped

- 1 ¼ cups packed light brown sugar

- 2 tablespoons cider vinegar

- 1 tablespoon lime zest

- 3 tablespoons lime juice

- ½ teaspoon salt

- ½ teaspoon crushed red pepper

- 4 whole cloves

- 1 cinnamon stick

Directions

1. Combine tomatoes, brown sugar, vinegar, lime zest, lime juice, salt, crushed red pepper, cloves and cinnamon stick in a large nonreactive saucepan; bring to a boil over medium-high heat. Reduce heat to low and simmer, stirring occasionally, until the mixture thickens and becomes syrupy, 50 to 60 minutes. Remove and discard the cinnamon stick and cloves.

2. Working in batches, if needed, pour the tomato mixture into a blender. Secure the lid on the blender and remove the center piece to allow steam to escape. Place a clean towel over the opening. Process until mostly smooth, 5 to 10 seconds. (Use caution when blending hot liquids.) Transfer to a pint-size mason jar. Let stand, uncovered, to cool to room temperature, about 1 hour. Screw on the lid and refrigerate until completely cold, about 2 hours.

Pear Jam

Ingredients

- 1 ½ pounds Bartlett pears, peeled and chopped

- ¼ cup light brown sugar

- ¼ cup honey

- 1 tablespoon lemon juice

- 1 teaspoon grated fresh ginger

- ¼ teaspoon ground cardamom

- ¼ teaspoon salt

- ⅛ teaspoon ground cloves

- 1 cinnamon stick

Directions

1. Combine pears, brown sugar, honey, lemon juice, ginger, cardamom, salt, cloves and cinnamon stick in a large saucepan. Cook over medium heat, stirring occasionally, until the pears start to release juices, about 5 minutes. Increase

heat to medium-high and cook, stirring occasionally, until thickened (or until a candy thermometer registers 220 degrees F), 20 to 25 minutes.

2. Remove from heat; discard the cinnamon stick. Using a potato masher, mash the mixture to the desired consistency. Let cool completely, about 1 hour. Divide the jam between two 8-ounce jars. Use immediately, or cover and refrigerate for up to 3 weeks.

Tips

To make ahead: Cover and refrigerate for up to 3 weeks.

Plum Jam

Ingredients

- 2 pounds black or red plums, cored and roughly chopped

- 1 cup granulated sugar

- 2 tablespoons orange juice

- ¼ teaspoon salt

Directions

1. Combine plums, sugar, orange juice and salt in a large saucepan. Cook over medium heat, stirring occasionally, until the plums start to release their juices, about 5 minutes. Increase heat to medium-high and cook, stirring occasionally, until thickened (or until a candy thermometer registers

220 degrees F), 20 to 25 minutes. Remove from heat.

2. Using a potato masher, mash the mixture to the desired consistency. Let cool completely, about 1 hour. Divide the jam between two 8-ounce jars. Use immediately, or cover and refrigerate for up to 3 weeks.

Tips

To make ahead: Cover and refrigerate for up to 3 weeks.

Blood Oranges with Rose Water & Pistachios

Ingredients

- 8 medium blood oranges and/or navel oranges

- 2 tablespoons dark amber agave syrup

- ¼ teaspoon rose water (see Tip) or vanilla extract

- ⅓ cup chopped lightly salted pistachios or slivered almonds, toasted

Directions

1. Slice ends off oranges. Using a sharp knife, remove and discard the peel and white pith. Cut the oranges crosswise into 1/4-inch-thick slices. Remove any seeds. Arrange the slices on a platter, overlapping slightly.

2. Mix agave syrup with rose water (or vanilla) in a small bowl. Drizzle over the oranges and sprinkle with pistachios (or almonds).

To make ahead

Refrigerate sliced oranges and syrup mixture separately for up to 3 days.

Tip

A bottle of rose water should last a very long time because a little goes a long way. It is made by distilling rose petals in water to release their essence and is used throughout the Middle East and Mediterranean in sweets like baklava and in drinks. Find it in well-stocked grocery stores and gourmet markets.

Blackberry Jam

Ingredients

- 3 pounds fresh or frozen blackberries

- 2 cups granulated sugar

- ¼ cup fresh lime juice

- 1 ½ tablespoons grated fresh ginger

- ¼ teaspoon salt

Directions

1. Combine blackberries and sugar in a large saucepan. Let stand for 1 hour, stirring occasionally.

2. Place the blackberry mixture over medium-high heat; bring to a boil, stirring often and mashing the berries with the back of a spoon to help break them down, until the mixture is thick and jammy, 15 to 20 minutes. Set a fine-mesh strainer over a large heatproof bowl. Strain half of the blackberry mixture, pressing with the back of the spoon to extract remaining juices. Return the strained

blackberry juice to the saucepan; discard the solids in the strainer.

3. Reduce heat to medium-low; place a candy thermometer in the pan. Stir in lime juice, ginger and salt. Continue to cook, stirring constantly, until the mixture reaches 220°F, 15 to 20 minutes more. (The jam is ready when the bubbles become more stable and the mixture is thickened enough that you can see the bottom of the saucepan when you stir.) Remove from heat and let stand for 10 minutes.

4. Ladle the jam evenly among 4 (1-pint) clean canning jars and place lids on the jars. Let stand at room temperature until completely cooled, about 3 hours.

Chapter 5: Savory Sauces and Condiments

Blueberry Ketchup

Ingredients

- 2 ½ cups fresh blueberries
- 1 medium shallot, minced (about 2 tablespoons)
- 1 ¼ cups sugar
- ½ cup red-wine vinegar
- 2 tablespoons minced fresh ginger
- 1 tablespoon lime juice
- ¼ teaspoon salt
- ¼ teaspoon freshly ground pepper

Directions

1. Place blueberries, sugar, vinegar, ginger, lime juice, salt and pepper in a large saucepan over medium-high heat. Stir until the sugar dissolves,

about 5 minutes. Bring to a simmer, reduce heat to medium-low and simmer, stirring occasionally, until the blueberries have mostly broken down and the sauce has thickened, 20 to 30 minutes. Spoon into glass jars or a large bowl and refrigerate until chilled and thickened, about 4 hours.

Tips

Make Ahead Tip: Cover and refrigerate for up to 2 weeks or freeze for up to 1 month.

To oil a grill rack, oil a folded paper towel, hold it with tongs and rub it over the rack. (Do not use cooking spray on a hot grill.)

Cranberry Relish

Ingredients

- 6 pitted medjool dates

- ½ small shallot

- 4 sage leaves

- 1 medium orange, quartered and seeded

- 2 cups fresh cranberries, thawed if frozen

- 2 tablespoons brown sugar

Directions

1. Place dates, shallot and sage in a food processor and process for 20 seconds. Add cranberries and orange and pulse until combined into a coarse relish. Serve at room temperature or cold.

Tips

Make Ahead Tip: Cover and refrigerate for up to 3 days.

Orange-Sesame Dressing

Ingredients

- ¼ cup orange juice

- ¼ cup cider vinegar

- 2 tablespoons sugar

- 2 tablespoons reduced-sodium soy sauce

- 1 teaspoon toasted sesame oil

Directions

1. Combine orange juice, vinegar, sugar, soy sauce and oil in a small bowl or jar with a tight-fitting lid. Whisk or shake until the sugar has dissolved.

Tips

People with celiac disease or gluten-sensitivity should use soy sauces that are labeled "gluten-free," as soy sauce may contain wheat or other gluten-containing sweeteners and flavors.

Orange-Miso Sauce

Ingredients

- 1/4 cup sweet white miso, (see Ingredient notes)

- 1 tablespoon orange zest

- ¼ cup orange juice

- 1/4 cup flaxseed oil, (see Ingredient notes) or canola oil

- 1 tablespoon minced fresh ginger

- 1 tablespoon rice vinegar

- 1 teaspoon mirin, (optional)

Directions

1. Combine miso, orange zest and juice, oil, ginger, rice vinegar and mirin (if using) in a small bowl and whisk until thoroughly blended.

Tips

Ingredient Notes: Made from fermented soybeans, miso is a common ingredient in Japanese cooking. There are different types of miso, in shades ranging from white and yellow to reddish brown and dark brown. Available at health-food stores and Japanese markets.

Flaxseed oil, pressed from flaxseeds, is a valued as a source of omega-3 fatty acids. It is highly perishable, so store in the refrigerator and use as soon as possible. Available at natural-foods stores.

Roasted Cherry Tomato & Sage Sauce

Ingredients

- 2 pints cherry tomatoes

- 1 medium onion, thinly sliced

- 4 cloves garlic, minced

- ¼ cup chopped fresh sage

- 3 tablespoons extra-virgin olive oil, divided

- 1 tablespoon red-wine vinegar

- ½ teaspoon salt

- ¼ teaspoon freshly ground pepper

Directions

1. Preheat oven to 450 degrees F.

2. Combine tomatoes, onion, garlic, sage, 1 tablespoon oil, vinegar, salt and pepper in a 9-by-13-inch metal pan. Roast, stirring once halfway through, until the tomatoes and onion are tender, 15 to 20 minutes.

3. Lightly mash the tomatoes to release their juices. Stir in the remaining 2 tablespoons oil. Serve warm.

Tips

Make Ahead Tip: Cover and refrigerate for up to 3 days; reheat before using.

Blueberry-Bourbon Barbecue Sauce

Ingredients

- 1 tablespoon canola oil

- 1 small red onion, chopped

- 4 cloves garlic, chopped

- 1-2 jalapenos, seeded and chopped

- ½ cup bourbon

- 2 cups fresh or frozen (not thawed) blueberries

- ½ cup ketchup

- ⅓ cup cider vinegar

- 2 tablespoons brown sugar

- 1 tablespoon molasses

- ⅛ teaspoon ground allspice

Directions

1. Heat oil in a large saucepan over medium heat. Add onion and cook, stirring occasionally, until tender and just starting to brown, 2 to 4 minutes. Add garlic and jalapeno and cook, stirring, until fragrant, about 30 seconds. Add bourbon, increase heat to high and bring to a boil; cook until most of the liquid has evaporated, about 5 minutes. Stir in blueberries, ketchup, vinegar, brown sugar, molasses and allspice; return to a boil. Reduce the heat and simmer, stirring occasionally, until thickened, about 20 minutes.

Tips

Make Ahead Tip: Cover and refrigerate for up to 2 weeks or freeze for up to 3 months.

Lemon-Mint Vinaigrette

Ingredients

- ⅓ cup lemon juice

- 1 tablespoon Dijon mustard

- 1 teaspoon sugar

- 1 clove garlic, minced

- ⅓ cup extra-virgin olive oil

- ⅓ cup chopped fresh mint

- ⅛ teaspoon salt

- Freshly ground pepper, to taste

Directions

1. Whisk lemon juice, mustard, sugar and garlic in a small bowl until blended. Drizzle in oil, whisking until blended. Stir in mint, salt and pepper.

Avocado Mayo

Ingredients

- ½ ripe avocado, mashed

- 2 tablespoons mayonnaise

- 1 scallion, finely chopped

- ½ teaspoon lime zest

Directions

1. Combine avocado, mayonnaise, scallion and lime zest in a small bowl.

Tips

Make Ahead Tip: Press plastic wrap directly on the surface and refrigerate for up to 4 hours.

Spicy Herb Sauce

Ingredients

• 5 cups tender fresh herbs, such as basil, cilantro and/or parsley, tough stems removed

• 2 tablespoons woody fresh herb leaves, such as thyme, rosemary and/or sage

• ½ cup chopped jalapeño peppers, seeded if desired

• 2 cloves garlic, smashed and peeled

• 1 cup grapeseed or avocado oil

- 1 tablespoon lemon or lime juice

- 1 ½ teaspoons salt

Directions

1. Combine tender and woody herbs, jalapeños and garlic in a food processor. Pulse, scraping down the sides occasionally, until finely chopped. With the motor running, slowly add oil. Add lemon (or lime) juice and salt and pulse to combine. Serve immediately or transfer to an airtight container and refrigerate for up to 1 week or freeze for up to 6 months.

Tips

To make ahead: Refrigerate for up to 1 week or freeze for up to 6 months.

Zhoug Sauce

Ingredients

- 1 cup packed fresh cilantro leaves

- 1 cup packed fresh flat-leaf parsley leaves

- ¼ cup lemon juice

- 2 large jalapeños, chopped

- 2 cloves garlic, chopped

- 1 teaspoon ground coriander

- 1 teaspoon ground cumin

- ½ teaspoon salt

- ¼ cup extra-virgin olive oil

Directions

1. Combine cilantro, parsley, lemon juice, jalapeños, garlic, coriander, cumin and salt in a food processor. Process until finely chopped. With the motor running, slowly add oil; process until well combined.

Tips

To make ahead: Omit lemon juice and refrigerate for up to 3 days. Stir in lemon juice just before serving.

No-Peel Slow-Cooker Marinara Sauce

Ingredients

- 6 pounds tomatoes

- 2 cups chopped onion

- ¼ cup extra-virgin olive oil

- 1 (6 ounce) can tomato paste

- 3 tablespoons finely chopped garlic

- 2 tablespoons finely chopped fresh oregano

- 2 tablespoons balsamic vinegar

- 4 teaspoons granulated sugar

- 1 ½ teaspoons salt, divided

- 1 teaspoon Ground pepper or crushed red pepper to taste

Directions

1. Cut tomatoes in half crosswise. Gently squeeze out the seeds and discard (don't worry if you don't get them all). Mix onion, oil, tomato paste, garlic, oregano, vinegar, sugar and 1 teaspoon salt in a 6-quart or larger slow cooker. Place the tomatoes on top.

2. Cover and cook for 2 hours on High or 4 hours on Low.

3. Puree with an immersion blender or in a regular blender in batches until chunky. (Use caution when pureeing hot liquids.) Placing the lid askew, cook until thickened, about 3 hours more on High or 6 hours more on Low.

4. Season with the remaining 1/2 teaspoon salt and pepper (or crushed red pepper) to taste. Puree further, if desired. Serve hot or let cool completely

before refrigerating for up to 5 days or freezing for up to 6 months.

Tips

To make ahead: Refrigerate for up to 5 days or freeze for up to 6 months.

Equipment: 6-qt. or larger slow cooker

Avocado Pesto

Ingredients

- 1 large bunch fresh basil

- 2 ripe avocados

- ½ cup walnuts or hemp seeds

- 2 tablespoons lemon juice

- 3 cloves garlic

- ½ teaspoon fine sea salt

- ½ cup extra-virgin olive oil

- Ground pepper, to taste

Directions

1. Strip basil leaves from the stems and add to a food processor along with avocados, walnuts (or hemp seeds), lemon juice, garlic and salt; pulse until finely chopped. Add oil and process to form a thick paste. Season with pepper.

Homemade Tomato Sauce

Ingredients

- 4 pounds tomatoes, cored, halved, and seeded

- 1 red bell pepper, halved and seeded

- 2 tablespoons olive oil, divided

- 1 cup chopped sweet onion

- 4 cloves garlic, minced

- 1 tablespoon white balsamic vinegar

- ¼ teaspoon salt

- ¼ teaspoon ground pepper

- ½ cup chopped fresh basil, Italian parsley, and/or oregano

Directions

1. Preheat broiler. Lightly brush tomatoes and bell pepper with 1 tablespoon of the oil. Arrange half of the tomatoes and the pepper, cut sides down, in

a 15x10-inch baking pan. Broil 5 to 6 inches from heat 8 to 10 minutes or until charred. Remove from pan; wrap pepper in foil. Repeat with the remaining tomatoes. Let tomatoes and pepper stand 20 minutes or until cool enough to handle. Peel off and discard skins. Chop tomatoes and pepper; set aside.

2. Heat the remaining 1 tablespoon oil in a large saucepan over medium heat. Add onion and garlic; cook 5 to 7 minutes or until onion is tender, stirring occasionally. Add reserved tomatoes and bell pepper, vinegar, salt and ground pepper. Bring to boiling; reduce heat. Simmer, uncovered, 20 to 30 minutes or until tomatoes have broken down and mixture is slightly thick, stirring occasionally. Cool slightly. Blend with an

immersion blender until smooth. Return to saucepan; heat through. Stir in herbs.

Tips

To make ahead: Transfer the sauce to a freezer container, let cool, and freeze up to 3 months. To use frozen sauce, thaw overnight in refrigerator. Reheat in a medium saucepan over medium-low until heated through. Use as desired.

Chapter 6: Hearty Soups and Stews

Chilled Strawberry-Rhubarb Soup

Ingredients

- 4 cups 1/2-inch pieces rhubarb, fresh or frozen

- 3 cups water

- 1 ½ cups sliced strawberries

- ¼ cup sugar

- ⅛ teaspoon salt

- ⅓ cup chopped fresh basil or mint, plus more for garnish

- Freshly ground pepper to taste

Directions

1. Bring rhubarb and 3 cups water to a boil in a large saucepan. Cook until the rhubarb is very soft and broken down, about 5 minutes. Transfer to a medium bowl. Put a couple inches of ice water in a large bowl and set the bowl with the rhubarb in it to help cool it quickly. (If you aren't in a hurry, you can skip the ice-water bath.) Refrigerate, stirring occasionally, until cool, at least 20 minutes.

2. Transfer the rhubarb to a blender. Add strawberries, sugar and salt; blend until smooth. Return to the bowl and stir in 1/3 cup basil (or mint). Serve sprinkled with more herbs and a generous grinding of pepper.

Tips

To make ahead: Cover and refrigerate the soup (without basil or mint) for up to 1 day. Stir in herbs just before serving.

Persian-Style Butternut Squash Soup

Ingredients

- 4-5 saffron threads (see Tips)

- 2 tablespoons hot water

- 3 tablespoons olive oil

- 1 medium red onion, chopped

- 2 cloves garlic, chopped

- 1 medium butternut squash (about 2 3/4 pounds), peeled, seeded and cubed (1/2-inch)

- 1 large sweet potato (about 8 ounces), peeled and cubed (1/2-inch)

- ¾ teaspoon ground cumin

- ½ teaspoon kosher salt

- ½ teaspoon ground cinnamon

- ¼ teaspoon ground coriander

- ¼ teaspoon ground pepper

- 3 ½ cups water

- 1-2 teaspoons pure maple syrup

- A few drops orange blossom water (optional)

- Ground sumac for serving (see Tips)

Directions

1. Grind saffron threads with a mortar and pestle to get 1/4 teaspoon ground saffron. Place the ground saffron in a small glass bowl. Add 2 tablespoons very hot (but not boiling) water. Stir, cover and set aside to steep.

2. Heat oil in a large pot over medium heat. Add onion; cook, stirring, until soft and translucent, 6 to 8 minutes. Add garlic; cook, stirring, for another 2 minutes. Add squash, sweet potato, cumin, salt, cinnamon, coriander and pepper. Stir to combine; cook, stirring occasionally, until fragrant, about 5 minutes.

3. Add 3 1/2 cups water to the pot; increase heat to high and bring to a boil. Reduce heat to medium-low and add the reserved saffron water. If there is saffron clinging to the side of the bowl, drizzle in a little more water, swish it around and add it to

the pot (this is precious stuff!). Stir to combine; cover and simmer until the squash and sweet potato are soft and cooked through, about 25 minutes. Taste the broth for seasoning and adjust as desired.

4. Transfer the soup to a blender and add maple syrup and orange blossom water, if using. (Start with 1 teaspoon maple syrup and just a drop or two of orange blossom water--and don't measure over the soup.) Puree until smooth (use caution when blending hot liquids). Taste and add more syrup and orange blossom water, if desired, but keep in mind the maple syrup and orange blossom water should not overwhelm the soup. Ladle into bowls and sprinkle with sumac, if desired.

Tips

Tips: Saffron adds flavor and golden color to a variety of Middle Eastern, African and European foods. Find it in the spice section of supermarkets, gourmet shops or at tienda.com. It will keep in an airtight container for several years.

The tart red berries of the Mediterranean sumac bush add fruity, sour flavor to many regional dishes. Find ground sumac in Middle Eastern markets, specialty-food shops and online.

To make ahead: Cover and refrigerate for up to 3 days or freeze for up to 3 months.

Fresh Tomato Soup

Ingredients

• 2 pounds tomatoes, cored and seeded (see Tip)

- 1 ½ cups coarsely chopped red sweet peppers

- 1 cup reduced-sodium vegetable or chicken broth

- ¼ cup chopped sweet onion

- ¼ cup snipped fresh basil

- 2 tablespoons heavy cream

- 1 tablespoon honey

- 1 Grilled Cheese Croutons (see Tip)

Directions

1. Working in batches, in a blender or food processor combine tomatoes, peppers, broth, onion, and basil. Cover and blend or process until

smooth. Transfer all of the pureed mixture to a large saucepan.

2. Cook over medium 5 to 6 minutes or until heated through. Stir in cream and honey. If desired, top servings with Grilled Cheese Croutons and additional basil. Serve warm (see Tip).

Tips

Tips: If fresh in-season tomatoes aren't available, you can substitute two 14.5-oz. cans whole tomatoes.

To make optional Grilled Cheese Croutons, sandwich together any type of bread and a good melting cheese. Brush the outside of bread with butter or oil and toast in a hot skillet or griddle until golden on each side. Cut into croutons.

On hot summer days, serve this soup cold. Prepare as directed, except omit cream. If desired, increase honey to 2 Tbsp. Cover and chill 2 to 24 hours. If desired, top each serving with cut-up cherry tomatoes, fresh basil leaves, and a drizzle of olive oil.

Variation: Roasted Tomato Soup: Prepare as directed, except line two 15x10-inch baking pans with foil. Preheat oven to 450 degrees F. Cut tomatoes in half crosswise. Seed tomatoes; arrange halves, cut sides down, in one of the prepared pans. Cut onion into 1/2-inch slices. Cut sweet peppers in half lengthwise; remove stems, seeds, and membranes. Arrange onion slices and pepper halves, cut sides down, in the remaining prepared pan. Drizzle with 3 to 4 tablespoons olive oil. Roast onion and peppers 20 minutes or until peppers are charred, turning onion slices once. Bring foil up around onion and peppers and fold edges together to enclose. Let stand 15 to 20 minutes or until cool enough to handle. Peel off and discard pepper skins. Preheat broiler. Broil tomatoes 4 inches from heat 4 minutes or until charred. Continue as directed in Step 1.

Butternut Squash Soup with Avocado & Chickpeas

Ingredients

- 1 15-ounce can Amy's Light-in-Sodium Butternut Squash Soup

- ¾ cup canned chickpeas, rinsed

- 1 tablespoon lime juice

- 1 teaspoon curry powder

- Pinch of salt

- 2 tablespoons diced avocado

- 1 tablespoon nonfat plain Greek yogurt

Directions

1. Heat soup in a small saucepan with chickpeas, lime juice, curry powder and salt. To serve, top with avocado and yogurt.

Loaded Black Bean Nacho Soup

Ingredients

- 1 (18 ounce) carton low-sodium black bean soup

- ¼ teaspoon smoked paprika

- ½ teaspoon lime juice

- ½ cup halved grape tomatoes

- ½ cup shredded cabbage or slaw mix

- 2 tablespoons crumbled cotija cheese or other Mexican-style shredded cheese

- ½ medium avocado, diced

- 2 ounces baked tortilla chips

Directions

1. Pour soup into a small saucepan and stir in paprika. Heat according to package Directions. Stir in lime juice.

2. Divide the soup between 2 bowls and top with tomatoes, cabbage (or slaw), cheese and avocado. Serve with tortilla chips.

Spicy Weight-Loss Cabbage Soup Recipe

Ingredients

- 2 tablespoons extra-virgin olive oil

- 2 cups chopped onions

- 1 cup chopped carrot

- 1 cup chopped celery

- 1 cup chopped poblano or green bell pepper

- 4 large cloves garlic, minced

- 8 cups sliced cabbage

- 1 tablespoon tomato paste

- 1 tablespoon minced chipotle chiles in adobo sauce

- 1 teaspoon ground cumin

- ½ teaspoon ground coriander

- 4 cups low-sodium vegetable broth or chicken broth

- 4 cups water

- 2 (15 ounce) cans low-sodium pinto or black beans, rinsed

- ¾ teaspoon salt

- ½ cup chopped fresh cilantro, plus more for serving

- 2 tablespoons lime juice

- Crumbled queso fresco, nonfat plain Greek yogurt and/or diced avocado for garnish

Directions

1. Heat oil in a large soup pot (8 quart or larger) over medium heat. Add onions, carrot, celery, poblano (or bell pepper) and garlic; cook, stirring frequently, until softened, 10 to 12 minutes. Add cabbage; cook, stirring occasionally until slightly softened, about 10 minutes more. Add tomato paste, chipotle, cumin and coriander; cook, stirring, for 1 minute more.

2. Add broth, water, beans and salt. Cover and bring to a boil over high heat. Reduce heat and simmer, partially covered, until the vegetables are

tender, about 10 minutes. Remove from heat and stir in cilantro and lime juice. Serve garnished with cheese, yogurt and/or avocado, if desired.

Spicy Ramen Noodle Cup Soup Packs 16g Protein

Ingredients

- 1 ½ tablespoons reduced-sodium vegetable bouillon paste

- 1 ½ teaspoons white miso

- 1 ½ teaspoons chile-garlic sauce

- 1 ½ teaspoons grated ginger

- ¾ cup shredded carrot

- ¾ cup sliced shiitake mushrooms

- 1 ½ cups chopped baby spinach

- 3 hard-boiled eggs, halved

- 1 ½ cups cooked ramen noodles

- 3 tablespoons sliced scallions

- ¾ teaspoon sesame seeds

- 3 cups very hot water, divided

Directions

1. Place 1/2 tablespoon bouillon paste, 1/2 teaspoon miso, 1/2 teaspoon chili-garlic sauce and 1/2 teaspoon ginger in each of 3 pint-and-a-half size canning jars. Layer 1/4 cup carrot, 1/4 cup mushrooms, 1/2 cup spinach, 2 egg halves and 1/2 cup noodles in each jar. Top each with 1

tablespoon scallions and 1/4 teaspoon sesame seeds. Close the jars. Refrigerate for up to 3 days.

2. To make one jar of noodles, add 1 cup of very hot water to one jar. Close the jar and shake to combine. Microwave uncovered on high in 1-minute increments until steaming hot, 2 to 3 minutes. Let stand 5 minutes. Stir before eating.

Pasta e Fagioli with Instant Ramen Noodles

Ingredients

- 2 teaspoons extra-virgin olive oil

- 2 tablespoons finely chopped onion

- 1 medium carrot, peeled and finely chopped

- 1 celery stalk, finely chopped

- 2 cups water

- 1 cup no-salt-added canned diced tomatoes

- ½ teaspoon dried oregano

- 1 (3 ounce) package ramen-noodle soup mix

- 1 cup rinsed no-salt-added canned cannellini beans

- 2 tablespoons chopped fresh flat-leaf parsley

Directions

1. Heat oil in a medium saucepan over medium-high heat. Add onion, carrot and celery; cook, stirring occasionally, until beginning to soften, 3 to 5 minutes. Add water, tomatoes, oregano and 3/4 of the seasoning packet (discard the remainder or save for another use). Bring to a simmer.

2. Break noodles into bite-size pieces and add to the pan. Cook until tender, about 3 minutes. Stir in beans; cook until warmed. Divide between 2 bowls and sprinkle with parsley.

Hearty Tomato Soup with Beans & Greens

Ingredients

- 2 (14 ounce) cans low-sodium hearty-style tomato soup

- 1 tablespoon olive oil

- 3 cups chopped kale

- 1 teaspoon minced garlic

- ⅛ teaspoon crushed red pepper (Optional)

- 1 (14 ounce) can no-salt-added cannellini beans, rinsed

- ¼ cup grated Parmesan cheese

Directions

1. Heat soup in a medium saucepan according to package Directions; simmer over low heat as you prepare kale.

2. Heat oil in a large skillet over medium heat. Add kale and cook, stirring, until wilted, 1 to 2 minutes. Stir in garlic and crushed red pepper (if using) and cook for 30 seconds. Stir the greens and beans into the soup and simmer until the beans are heated through, 2 to 3 minutes.

3. Divide the soup among 4 bowls. Serve topped with Parmesan.

Egg Drop Soup with Instant Noodles, Spinach & Scallions

Ingredients

• 2 cups water

• ½ (3 ounce) package rice-noodle soup mix, such as Thai Kitchen Garlic & Vegetable

• 1 large egg

• 1 cup baby spinach

• 1 scallion, sliced

Directions

1. Bring water to a boil in a small saucepan. Stir in half of the seasoning packet (discard the remainder or reserve for another use). Add

noodles and cook until tender, about 3 minutes. Reduce heat to maintain a simmer.

2. Whisk egg in a small bowl. Slowly pour the egg into the simmering soup, stirring constantly. Fold in spinach until just wilted, about 30 seconds. Transfer to a bowl and sprinkle with scallion.

Immune Supporting Creamy Tomato Soup

Ingredients

- ¾ cup no-salt-added canned tomato puree

- ¼ cup low-sodium chicken broth

- 1 tablespoon reduced-fat cream cheese

Directions

1. Whisk tomatoes, broth and cream cheese in a large heatproof mug. Microwave on High, stirring occasionally, until heated through and creamy, about 2 minutes.

Chicken Curry Cup of Noodles

Ingredients

• 3 teaspoons reduced-sodium chicken bouillon paste, divided

• 6 teaspoons red curry paste, divided

• 6 tablespoons coconut milk, divided

• 1 ½ cups frozen stir-fry vegetable mix, divided

• 9 ounces chopped cooked boneless, skinless chicken breast, divided

- 1 ½ cups spiralized zucchini noodles, divided

- 3 teaspoons chopped cilantro, divided

- 3 cups very hot water, divided

Directions

1. Add 1 teaspoon bouillon paste, 2 teaspoons curry paste and 2 tablespoons coconut milk to each of three 1 1/2-pint canning jars. Layer 1/2 cup vegetables, 3 ounces chicken and 1/2 cup noodles in each jar. Top each with 1 teaspoon cilantro. Cover and refrigerate for up to 3 days.

2. To prepare one jar of noodles: Add 1 cup very hot water to a jar. Cover and shake to combine. Uncover and microwave on High in 1-minute increments until steaming hot, 2 to 3 minutes total. Let stand 5 minutes. Stir before eating.

Curried Butternut Squash Soup with Crispy Halloumi

Ingredients

• 1 (32 ounce) carton low-sodium butternut squash soup

• 1 teaspoon curry powder

• 4 ounces halloumi cheese, sliced into 1/2-inch pieces

• 1 teaspoon olive oil

• 4 teaspoons toasted pepitas

Directions

1. Heat soup according to package Directions. Whisk in curry powder and simmer for 3 minutes.

2. Pat cheese slices dry with a paper towel. Brush both sides with oil. Sear in a heavy pan over medium-high heat until golden brown, 1 to 2 minutes per side.

3. Serve the soup topped with the cheese and pepitas.

Creamy Roasted Vegetable Soup with Chicken

Ingredients

• 1 1/3 cups leftover Roasted Butternut Squash & Root Vegetables

• ½ cup light coconut milk

• ⅛ teaspoon garlic powder

• Pinch of salt

• Pinch of ground pepper

• 1/2 cup leftover chicken from Chicken Kebabs with Warm Cabbage-Apple Slaw, warmed and coarsely chopped

Directions

1. Combine vegetables, coconut milk, garlic powder, salt and pepper in a blender or food processor. Puree until smooth, adding 1 to 2 tablespoons water if needed to reach desired consistency.

2. Transfer the vegetable mixture to a small saucepan. Cook over medium heat, stirring frequently, until heated through, 3 to 5 minutes. Top with chicken.

Chapter 7: Healthy Snack and Meal Starters

Jalapeno-Cranberry Relish

Ingredients

• 1 12-ounce bag cranberries, fresh or frozen (thawed)

• 1 teaspoon lime zest

• 2 teaspoons lime juice

• 1-2 fresh jalapeños, seeded and coarsely chopped

• 2 tablespoons minced red onion

• ⅓ cup sugar

• 2 tablespoons extra-virgin olive oil

- Pinch of salt

Directions

1. Combine cranberries, lime zest, lime juice, jalapeno to taste, onion, sugar, oil and salt in a food processor. Pulse until coarsely chopped. Let stand until the sugar has dissolved, about 10 minutes. Transfer to a serving dish. Serve at room temperature or cover and refrigerate until cold.

Tips

Make Ahead Tip: Cover and refrigerate for up to 2 days.

Quick & Easy Pickled Cabbage

Ingredients

- 1 ½ cups water

- ½ cup rice vinegar or white vinegar

- ¼ cup granulated sugar

- 2 tablespoons salt

- 5 cups thinly shredded green or red cabbage (from 1 small head)

- 2 medium shallots, thinly sliced (about 1/2 cup)

- 1 medium red Fresno or jalapeño pepper, seeded and thinly sliced

- 2 fresh thyme sprigs

Directions

1. Combine water, vinegar, sugar and salt in a large pot; bring to a boil over medium-high heat.

Immediately add cabbage, shallots and chile. Immediately remove from heat; stir and let cool completely, about 45 minutes. (The vegetables should be submerged in the liquid. If not, pack the mixture into the jar to marinate and cool at the same time. Keep the lid off the jar until the mixture is completely cooled, about 1 hour.)

2. Pack the cooled mixture into a 1-quart glass jar; place thyme sprigs into the side of the jar. Cover tightly and refrigerate for at least 24 hours.

Equipment

1-quart glass jar with lid

To make ahead

Refrigerate for up to 2 weeks.

Homemade Kombucha

Ingredients

- 1 gallon water

- 1 cup sugar

- 6 plain black tea bags

- 1 kombucha SCOBY (see Tip)

- 1 cup starter kombucha (see Tip)

Directions

1. Bring water to a boil in a large pot. Once boiling, remove from heat and stir in sugar, then add tea bags.

2. Allow the tea to cool to room temperature, 2 to 3 hours. Remove the tea bags, then pour the tea into a 1-gallon glass jar. Gently pour SCOBY and starter kombucha into the jar.

3. Cover the jar with a paper towel or clean tea towel and affix it with a rubber band. Place the jar in a warm (the ideal temperature is 75°F), dark location until it is tangy and fruity, about 8 days. Avoid cool locations, which can lead to mold. Note: During fermenting, the SCOBY may float on top or sink to the bottom and, after a few days, a new SCOBY layer will form.

4. After 8 days, taste the kombucha for doneness. If it tastes sweeter than you prefer, allow the kombucha to ferment for another day or two. If necessary, continue tasting for up to 14 days until the desired flavor is reached.

5. When the kombucha is done, remove the SCOBY and place it in a sealable container with 1 cup of the kombucha to store. (Store it, refrigerated, for up to 2 weeks until you're ready to make the next batch of kombucha. If, over time, the SCOBY grows several layers thick, remove a layer and discard it, or share it with a friend.)

6. Pour the kombucha through a fine-mesh strainer into a pitcher or large measuring cup(s) to filter out any sediment. Using a funnel, pour the kombucha into sealable glass bottles.

7. Close the bottles and return them to the warm, dark storage location until carbonated, 1 to 2 weeks.

Equipment

1-gallon glass jar, paper towel or clean tea towel, rubber band, funnel, fine-mesh strainer, sealable glass bottles

Tip

Kombucha SCOBY is widely available online. Starter kombucha is simply kombucha from a previous batch. If this is your first time making kombucha, starter kombucha will be included with your purchased SCOBY.

Quick Pickled Turnips

Ingredients

- 3-4 small turnips (about 12 ounces), peeled and very thinly sliced

- ½ cup quartered and thinly sliced red onion

- 3 cloves garlic, smashed and peeled

- 1 cup white-wine vinegar

- 1 cup hot water

- 1 tablespoon sugar

- 10 whole black peppercorns

- 1 teaspoon salt

- 1/4-1/2 teaspoon crushed red pepper (optional)

Directions

1. Layer turnips, onion and garlic in a quart jar (or similar 4-cup container) with a lid.

2. Whisk vinegar, hot water, sugar, peppercorns, salt and crushed red pepper (if using) in a medium bowl until the sugar is mostly dissolved. Pour the

mixture over the vegetables. Put the lid on and gently shake a few times to distribute the flavorings. Refrigerate for at least 30 minutes for the flavors to develop.

Tips

Make Ahead Tip: Cover and refrigerate for up to 2 weeks.

Jardiniere

Ingredients

- 2 ½ teaspoons coriander seeds

- 2 ½ teaspoons fennel seeds

- ¾ teaspoon black peppercorns

- 3 ¾ cups white-wine vinegar

- 1 ¾ cups water

- 2 ½ tablespoons kosher salt

- ⅓ cup honey

- 2 cups small cauliflower florets

- 2 cups trimmed and halved green beans

- 2 cups sliced mixed bell peppers

- 2 cups sliced yellow squash

- 1 ¼ cups sliced carrots

- 1 chile pepper, such as Fresno or bird's eye, thinly sliced

Directions

1. Toast coriander and fennel seeds in a small skillet over medium-low heat, stirring often, until golden and fragrant, about 2 minutes. Transfer to a mortar and add peppercorns. Crush with a pestle until coarsely cracked. (Alternatively, use a spice grinder.)

2. Combine vinegar, water and salt in a large saucepan. Bring to a boil over high heat. Remove from heat and whisk in honey and the spices.

3. Divide cauliflower, green beans, bell peppers, squash, carrots and chile between two 2-quart (or among four 1-quart) glass jars. Pour the warm brine over the vegetables to cover. Trim the vegetables, if necessary, so they are submerged in the brine. Let cool to room temperature, then cover and refrigerate for at least 8 hours or up to three weeks.

Sweet Pickled Peppers

Ingredients

• 2 pounds hot peppers, sliced or halved (about 8 cups)

• 3 cups distilled white vinegar or cider vinegar

• 3 cups water

• 1 ½ cups sugar

• 1 tablespoon plus 1 teaspoon sea salt

Directions

1. Place a large bowl of ice water next to the stove. Bring a large pot of water to a boil in a large pot. Add half of the peppers, cover, return to a boil and cook for 2 minutes. Use a slotted spoon to transfer

the peppers to the ice water to cool. Repeat with the remaining peppers. Drain the cooled peppers and divide among 6 pint-size (2-cup) canning jars or similar-size tempered-glass or heatproof-plastic containers with lids.

2. Combine vinegar, 3 cups water, sugar and salt in a large saucepan. Bring to a boil and stir until the sugar and salt dissolve. Boil for 2 minutes. Remove from the heat.

3. Carefully fill jars (or containers) with brine to within 1/2 inch of the rim, covering the peppers completely. (Discard any leftover brine.)

4. Place the lids on the jars (or containers). Refrigerate for at least 24 hours before serving. Store in the refrigerator for up to 1 month.

Tips

Make Ahead Tip: Cover and refrigerate for up to 1 month.

Equipment: 6 pint-size (2-cup) canning jars or similar-size tempered-glass or heatproof-plastic containers with lids

Tomato-Pepper Relish

Ingredients

- ¼ cup extra-virgin olive oil

- 12 cups diced bell peppers (about 3 1/2 pounds)

- 5 cups diced yellow onions (about 1 1/2 pounds)

- 12 cloves garlic, sliced

- 1 tablespoon crushed red pepper

- 1 tablespoon kosher salt

- 16 cups diced tomatoes (about 7 pounds)

- 1 ¼ cups dark brown sugar

- 1 ¼ cups red-wine vinegar

- 4 bay leaves

Directions

1. Heat oil in a large pot over medium heat. Add peppers, onions, garlic, crushed red pepper and salt. Cook, stirring occasionally, until softened, 10 to 12 minutes. Add tomatoes plus all their accumulated liquid, brown sugar, vinegar and bay leaves. Bring to a boil over high heat, then reduce

heat to maintain a lively simmer. Cook until reduced by half, about 2 1/2 hours.

2. Ladle into 7 sterilized pint-size jars (see Tips). Leave about 1/2 inch of headspace. Wipe the rims with a clean cloth. Place lids and rings on the jars. Twist until just finger-tight (won't move with gentle finger pressure), but don't overtighten. If canning, process in a hot water bath for 10 minutes (see Tips). Otherwise, let cool to room temperature and refrigerate.

Tips

To make ahead: Refrigerate for up to 1 month. If canned, store at room temperature for up to 1 year.

Equipment: 7 pint-size (16 oz.) canning jars with lids

Tips: Wash jars, lids and bands in hot, soapy water. Rinse well; dry the bands. Place the rack in the canning pot and place the jars, right-side up, on the rack. Add enough water to cover the jars by at least 1 inch. Cover the pot and bring to a simmer over medium heat. Turn off the heat, but keep the jars in the hot water, covered, until ready to use.

When the recipe is ready, remove the jars from the hot water with the jar lifter, pour out any water, and place on a towel (if placed directly on a cold surface, the jars could crack). Add vegetables or pickle recipes to the jars. Use the funnel to fill jars with brine, leaving 1/2 inch of headspace and making sure the liquid covers the vegetables. Run a chopstick around the inside of the jars to release any air bubbles. Wipe the rims with a clean towel. Add lids and rings and tighten until just finger-tight (won't move with gentle pressure), but don't overtighten.

Drunken Prunes

Ingredients

• 2 heaping teaspoons Darjeeling or other black tea leaves

• 2 cups boiling water

• ½ cup packed light brown sugar

• 1 1/4 pounds pitted prunes, (dried plums)

• 1 cup Armagnac, or cognac

• 1 vanilla bean, cut in half

Directions

1. Stir tea and water in a small bowl; let steep for 5 minutes. Strain into a medium saucepan; stir in brown sugar. Bring to a boil over high heat; boil until slightly thickened, about 2 minutes. Place prunes in a large bowl; stir in hot syrup. Set aside to cool to room temperature, about 1 hour.

2. Meanwhile, sterilize two 1-pint canning jars by steaming them upside down, their lids alongside, in a closed steamer for 10 minutes; or place in a large pot and cover by 1 inch of water and boil for 10 minutes.

3. Drain prunes, reserving liquid separately. Whisk Armagnac (or cognac) into the liquid. Pack each sterilized jar with half the prunes. Nestle half the vanilla bean in each jar. Pour 1/2 cup of the Armagnac mixture into each jar. Seal and turn upside down to blend Ingredients. Set right side

up and store in the refrigerator for 1 week to plump.

Tips

Tip

Refrigerate the prunes in sealed jars for up to 2 months. When giving, include a card with serving suggestions: "Spoon these 'drunken prunes' over vanilla frozen yogurt, mascarpone cheese or plain yogurt."

Sweet Pickled Green Beans

Ingredients

• 2 pounds green beans, stem ends trimmed (about 9 cups)

- 6-18 small whole dried chile peppers

- 3 cups distilled white vinegar or cider vinegar

- 3 cups water

- 1 ½ cups sugar

- 1 tablespoon plus 1 teaspoon sea salt

Directions

1. Place a large bowl of ice water next to the stove. Bring a large pot of water to a boil in a large pot. Add half of the green beans, cover, return to a boil and cook for 2 minutes. Use a slotted spoon to transfer the beans to the ice water to cool. Repeat with the remaining beans.

2. Drain the cooled beans and divide among 6 pint-size (2-cup) canning jars or similar-size tempered-

glass or heatproof-plastic containers with lids. Add 1 to 3 chile peppers to each jar.

3. Combine vinegar, 3 cups water, sugar and salt in a large saucepan. Bring to a boil and stir until the sugar and salt dissolve. Boil for 2 minutes. Remove from the heat.

4. Carefully fill jars (or containers) with brine to within 1/2 inch of the rim, covering the beans completely. (Discard any leftover brine.)

5. Place the lids on the jars (or containers). Refrigerate for at least 24 hours before serving. Store in the refrigerator for up to 1 month.

Tips

Make Ahead Tip: Cover and refrigerate for up to 1 month.

Equipment: 6 pint-size (2-cup) canning jars or similar-size tempered-glass or heatproof-plastic containers with lids

The Best Pickled Red Onions

Ingredients

- 1 cup white-wine vinegar

- ½ cup water

- 2 tablespoons granulated sugar

- 1 large clove garlic, very thinly sliced

- 1 bay leaf

- 2 (3-inch) thyme sprigs

- 1 teaspoon kosher salt

- ¼ teaspoon black peppercorns

- 2 ½ cups thinly sliced red onion

Directions

1. Combine vinegar, water, sugar, garlic, bay leaf, thyme, salt and peppercorns in a small saucepan. Bring to a boil over high heat, stirring until the sugar and salt are dissolved.

2. Meanwhile, place onion in a quart-size mason jar.

3. Pour the pickling liquid over the onion in the jar. Press the onion with the back of a wooden spoon to fully submerge it in the pickling liquid.

4. Let stand at room temperature for 30 minutes. Seal the lid. Refrigerate for at least 3 hours or up to 1 month.

To make ahead

Refrigerate in a sealed jar for up to 1 month, making sure onion is submerged in liquid.

Dilly Pickled Snap Peas

Ingredients

- 1 cup distilled white vinegar

- 1 cup water

- 2 tablespoons kosher salt

- 2 large cloves garlic, sliced

- 1 teaspoon dill seed

- 1 teaspoon mustard seed

- ½ teaspoon crushed red pepper

- 1 pound sugar snap peas, trimmed

- 1 tablespoon chopped fresh dill

Directions

1. Combine vinegar, water and salt in a large saucepan. Bring to a boil over medium-high heat. Cook, stirring, until the salt dissolves, about 2 minutes. Remove from heat and add garlic, dill seed, mustard seed and crushed red pepper. Add peas to the brine and let marinate, stirring occasionally, for 15 minutes. Drain. Toss the peas with dill.

Pickled Turnips

Ingredients

• 2 ½ pounds turnips, peeled and cut into 1/4- to 1/2-inch-thick wedges or sticks (about 8 cups)

• 6 slices peeled beet

• 3-6 whole large cloves garlic, sliced

• 3 cups distilled white vinegar or cider vinegar

• 3 cups water

• 2 tablespoons plus 2 teaspoons sea salt

• 2 tablespoons sugar

Directions

1. Divide turnips among 6 pint-size (2-cup) canning jars or similar-size tempered-glass or heatproof-plastic containers with lids. Add 1 beet slice to each jar (this dyes the pickles pink) and divide the garlic slices among the jars.

2. Combine vinegar, 3 cups water, salt and sugar in a large saucepan. Bring to a boil and stir until the salt and sugar dissolve. Boil for 2 minutes. Remove from the heat.

3. Carefully fill jars (or containers) with brine to within 1/2 inch of the rim, covering the turnips completely. (Discard any leftover brine.)

4. Place the lids on the jars (or containers). Refrigerate for at least 1 week before serving. Store in the refrigerator for up to 1 month.

Tips

Make Ahead Tip: Cover and refrigerate for up to 1 month.

Equipment: 6 pint-size (2-cup) canning jars or similar-size tempered-glass or heatproof-plastic containers with lids

Quick Pickles

Ingredients

- 1 ¼ pounds pickling cucumbers, trimmed and cut into 1/4-inch slices

- 1 ½ teaspoons salt

- 1 cup cider vinegar

- 1 cup white vinegar

- 1 cup light brown sugar

- 1 cup slivered onion

- 2 cloves garlic, slivered

- 1 teaspoon dill seed

- 1 teaspoon mustard seed

Directions

1. Place cucumber slices in a colander set in the sink. Sprinkle with salt; stir to combine. Let stand for 20 minutes. Rinse, drain and transfer to a large heatproof bowl.

2. Meanwhile, combine cider vinegar, white vinegar, brown sugar, onion, garlic, dill and mustard seed in a medium saucepan. Bring to a boil. Reduce heat and simmer for 10 minutes. Pour

the hot liquid over the cucumbers; stir to combine. Refrigerate for at least 10 minutes to bring to room temperature.

Pickled Asparagus

Ingredients

- 1 pound fresh asparagus, trimmed

- 3 cloves garlic, thinly sliced

- 2 teaspoons black peppercorns

- 2 sprigs dill

- 1 teaspoon crushed red pepper (Optional)

- 1 ¼ cups distilled white vinegar

- 1 ¼ cups water

- ½ cup sugar

- 2 tablespoons salt

Directions

1. Place asparagus spears tips-down in a 1-quart lidded jar. Add garlic, peppercorns, dill and crushed red pepper, if using.

2. Combine vinegar, water, sugar and salt in a small saucepan; bring to a boil over medium-high heat. Boil, stirring occasionally, until the sugar is dissolved, about 3 minutes. Remove from heat.

3. Carefully pour the vinegar mixture over the asparagus mixture in the jar; screw the lid on tightly. Immediately place in the refrigerator. Chill for at least 8 hours.

Tips

To make ahead: Refrigerate in a sealed jar for up to 2 weeks.

Pickled Eggs

Ingredients

- 1 15-ounce can beets

- 1 cup cider vinegar

- ½ cup sugar

- 2 teaspoons salt

- 2 bay leaves

- 4 whole cloves

- 1 medium onion, sliced into rings

- 6 large eggs

Directions

1. Drain liquid from beets into a small saucepan, reserving the beets for another use (for instance, use them for Grilled Buffalo Steak with Radicchio-Beet Skewers). Add vinegar, sugar, salt, bay leaves and cloves to the pan. Bring to a boil over medium-high heat, stirring occasionally, until the sugar dissolves. Pour the pickling liquid into a large deep bowl and stir in onions; set aside to cool for 1 hour.

2. Meanwhile, place eggs in a single layer in a saucepan; cover with water. Bring to a simmer over medium-high heat. Reduce heat to low, cover

and cook at the lowest simmer for 10 minutes. Pour off the hot water and run cold water over the eggs until they are completely cooled. Peel the eggs.

3. When the pickling liquid is cool, place the peeled eggs in a 4-cup container; pour the pickling liquid over the eggs, then spoon the onions on top. (The onions should hold the eggs under the liquid.) Cover and refrigerate for 24 hours.

4. Remove the eggs and onions from the pickling liquid. Refrigerate in an airtight container. Serve the onions (which are also delicious on burgers) alongside the eggs, if desired.

Tips

Make Ahead Tip: Once removed from the pickling liquid, the eggs will keep, in an airtight container, in the refrigerator for up to 3 days.

Spicy Pickled Carrots

Ingredients

• 3 cups white vinegar

• 1 cup water

• ¾ cup sugar

• 2 tablespoons pickling salt or fine sea salt (not iodized)

• 3 pounds small spring carrots, sliced on the diagonal 1/8 inch thick

• 1 medium red onion, sliced 1/8 inch thick

- 2 fresh jalapeños, sliced into rings 1/8 inch thick

- 2 teaspoons dried oregano, preferably Mexican, divided

- 2 teaspoons cumin seed, divided

- 2 large cloves garlic, halved

Directions

1. Before starting the recipe, gather the needed equipment (see Tips).

2. Prepare four 1-pint (2-cup) canning jars and lids: wash in hot soapy water and rinse well. Place the rack in the pot and place the jars, right-side up, on the rack. Add enough water to fill and cover the jars by at least 1 inch. Cover the pot and bring to a boil; boil, covered, for 10 minutes, then turn off the

heat. Keep the jars in the hot water (with the pot covered) while you prepare the recipe.

3. Meanwhile, place the new lids in a small saucepan, cover with water and bring to a gentle simmer. Very gently simmer for 10 minutes (taking care not to boil). Turn off the heat and keep the lids in the water until ready to use.

4. Combine vinegar, water, sugar and salt in a 6- to 8-quart nonreactive pot (see Tips) and bring to a boil. Stir until the sugar is dissolved. Add the carrots, onion and jalapeños; return to a boil. Remove from heat and let stand for 10 minutes.

5. Meanwhile, remove the sterilized jars from the water and place on a clean towel (if they're placed on a cold surface, the jars could crack). Place 1/2

teaspoon each oregano and cumin seed in each jar, along with half a garlic clove.

6. Fill the jars with the vegetables and pickling liquid to within 1/2 inch of the rim. Wipe the rims with a clean cloth. Use a lid wand (or tongs) to remove the lids from the hot water. Place lids and dry rings on the jars. Tighten until just finger-tight (won't move with gentle pressure) but don't overtighten.

7. To process the filled jars: Using a jar lifter, return the jars to the pot with the warm water, placing them on the rack without touching one another or the sides of the pot. If the water does not cover the jars by 1 to 2 inches, add boiling water as needed. Cover the pot and bring to a boil; boil for10 minutes, then turn off the heat, uncover the pot and leave the jars in the water for 5 minutes. Use

the jar lifter to transfer the jars to a towel, with some space between each jar. Let stand, without moving, for 24 hours. (If you do not want to process the jars in a boiling-water bath, you can refrigerate the pickles for up to 2 months.)

8. After 24 hours, unscrew the rings and test the seals by pressing lightly on the center of each lid. They should have a slight concave indentation and neither yield to your pressure nor pop back. If a seal is not complete, you can process again in boiling water or store any unsealed jars in the refrigerator.

Tips

To make ahead: Store at room temperature for up to 1 year if processed in a water bath.

Equipment: Four 1-pint (2-cup) canning jars; canning equipment

For this recipe, you will need the following canning equipment: Four 1-pint (2-cup) canning jars with rings and new lids; a canning pot with a rack or a large pot plus a heatproof rack that fits into the bottom of the pot; jar lifter; lid wand or tongs to help remove lids from hot water; and a clean cloth to wipe the jar rims. Canning equipment is available in hardware stores and at canningpantry.com (complete kits $43-$75).

Be sure to use a nonreactive pan, baking dish or bowl—stainless-steel, enamel-coated or glass—when cooking with acidic food (citrus, cranberries, tomatoes) to prevent the food from reacting with the pan. Reactive pans, such as aluminum and cast-iron, can impart off colors and/or flavors.

Ginger Pickled Carrots

Ingredients

- 14 ounces carrots

- 2 cups water

- 1 cup white-wine or cider vinegar

- ½ cup thinly sliced fresh ginger

- 1 tablespoon granulated sugar

- 1 tablespoon kosher salt

Directions

1. Peel carrots. Using the vegetable peeler, cut the carrots into thin ribbons. Place the carrot ribbons

in a large heatproof bowl and set a fine-mesh sieve over the bowl.

2. Combine water, vinegar, ginger, sugar and salt in a medium saucepan. Bring to a boil over medium-high heat. Cook until the sugar and salt are dissolved. Pour the brine through the sieve, making sure the carrots are completely immersed. Cover and let cool to room temperature, about 30 minutes.

3. Transfer the carrots and brine to a clean container, cover tightly and refrigerate for at least 2 hours or up to 2 weeks.

Tips

To make ahead: Refrigerate for up to 2 weeks.

Chapter 8: Final Thought

Healthy eating for prediabetes and diabetes not only helps to manage your blood glucose (blood sugar), but it also helps you have a better relationship with food. Intentional food choices like eating more non-starchy veggies, opting for lean meats or plant-based proteins, choosing quality carbohydrates, and low-fat versions of cheeses and dressings, will all help you meet your health goals—and they'll taste great too! It is not about one food, or one meal, it's about healthy eating over time. Food nourishes you so you stay healthy, but our food choices are also impacted by our memories, culture, and community.

Eating well is one of the primary things you can do to help control diabetes.

Do I have to follow a special diet?

There isn't one specific diabetes diet. Your doctor can work with you to design a meal plan. A meal plan is a guide that tells you what kinds of food to eat at meals and for snacks. The plan also tells you how much food to have. For most people who have diabetes (and those without), a healthy diet consists of:

- 40% to 60% of calories from carbohydrates

- 20% calories from protein

- 30% or fewer calories from fat

Your diet should also be low in cholesterol, low in salt, and low in added sugar.

Can I eat any sugar?

Yes. In recent years, doctors have learned that eating some sugar doesn't usually cause problems for most people who have diabetes—if it is part of a balanced diet. Just be careful about how much sugar you eat and try not to add sugar to foods.

What kinds of foods can I eat?

In general, at each meal you may have:

• 2 to 5 choices (or up to 60 grams) of carbohydrates

• 1 choice of protein

• A certain amount of fat

Talk to your doctor or dietitian for specific advice.

Carbohydrates are found in fruits, vegetables, beans, dairy foods, and starchy foods such as breads. Try to have fresh fruits rather than canned fruits, fruit juices, or dried fruit. You may eat fresh vegetables and frozen or canned vegetables. Condiments such as nonfat mayonnaise, ketchup, and mustard are also carbohydrates.

Protein is found in meat, poultry, fish, dairy products, beans, and some vegetables. Try to eat poultry and fish more often than red meat. Don't eat poultry skin. Also, trim extra fat from all meat. Choose nonfat or reduced-fat options when you eat dairy, such as cheeses and yogurts.

Not all fats are bad. It is important to know the differences between fats. **Unsaturated fats** are the "good" fats (nuts, fish, olive oil, canola oil, seeds, etc.). **Saturated fats** are less healthy. You should limit these in your diet. They include red meats, butter, lard, full-fat dairy products, dark-meat poultry, etc. **Trans fats** are the worst fats for you. These fats can be found in processed foods like crackers, snack foods, and most fast foods. To identify trans fats, check food labels for the words "partially hydrogenated."

Your doctor or dietitian will tell you how many grams of fat you may eat each day. When eating fat-free versions of foods (such as mayonnaise and butter), check the label to see how many grams of carbohydrates they contain. Keep in mind that these products often have added sugar.